HEAL THE MOTHER, HEAL THE CHILD

Other Books By Susy O'Hare

Diary of an ADHD Mum: Learning to Live, Love & Laugh
Parenting a Child with ADHD

HEAL THE MOTHER, HEAL THE CHILD

Shining a Light on the Shadows to Consciously Awaken Future Generations

SUSY O'HARE

Foreword by Dr. Nicole LePera

Cataloguing-in-Publication entry is available from the National Library Australia.

Softcover: 978-0-6489097-0-5
Hardcover: 978-0-6489097-1-2
E-book: 978-0-6489097-2-9

Available in hardcover, softcover, e-book, and audiobook

Cover photos Bronnie Joel Photography

To Seren, Daisy and Flynn—thank you.

CONTENTS

FOREWORD

I met Susy in the Instagram community a couple of years ago, and her posts and comments kept catching my eye. When I journeyed over to her Instagram page, my mind was blown—not only at the wealth of healing knowledge she was putting out to the world but also how she was embodying the work in her life.

Susy has done some incredible work around the powerful concept of 'Heal The Mother, Heal The Child'.

Instead of trying to fix her daughter, Susy discovered that first and foremost, she needed to fix herself and work on her healing. Susy understood that she needed to go on a journey of evolution, rebuild trust with herself, and begin to trust her intuition.

I commend her on paving the way for a new parenting paradigm where instead of trying to fix the child, we turn the light on our healing and begin from that place.

It can be a painful truth to take a long hard look at ourselves and see that often the behaviours our children are displaying are simply mirrored from our own unhealed and unprocessed pain. I believe a lot of parents are unintentionally making choices that are not even entirely theirs. We become habituated, we have these beliefs, and then we operate our decisions based on them. We are often not even conscious when we make these parenting choices. Instead, we are working with the information we have at the time, and we continue with those parenting patterns from our subconscious based on the way we were raised—even when those patterns didn't work for us.

Children need moments of fully present interconnectedness. If we cannot trust ourselves and our intuition, then we cannot extend it to our child. When things weren't great for us as children, we can doubt our abilities as parents, but we need to begin to trust ourselves, slow down, and connect once again with ourselves.

Conscious parenting is taking a moment to connect with our children truly, so they feel safe, seen, and heard. These are the universal core wants and desires of all humans, but especially children.

Susy's book will give you a framework to begin this healing work for mothers who are struggling with themselves and maybe even their children. It will bring you back to yourself, help you to be present, and help you trust the connection with your intuition so you can parent your child from that beautiful heart-space and not your childhood conditioning. You will begin to trust yourself instead of looking outside of yourself for decision-making about your child. You will discover that it was within you the whole time.

When our children or our partners trigger us, there is something deeper happening. Susy's book will teach mothers how to work on their triggers, explore their wounded egos, and begin to heal their inner child. They will find themselves less reactive and able to hold space for their children, allowing them to show up authentically as themselves. Mothers will then be able to let their child be seen, heard, and validated—without getting triggered by their inner child, as she is now met with love and acceptance.

Susy teaches us that we need not look at the child as an extension of ourselves; their behaviour is not a reflection of our capability as parents. We need to stop looking at what others think, but instead, go within and examine ourselves. We need to see our children as our mirrors and discover that their triggers can take us to our inner healing, which is beautiful. Our children then become our teachers.

The path into trusting intuition with parenting is first and foremost to reconnect and rebuild trust in one's self and one's healing. Heal yourself. Until you have reconnected with yourself, worked out what's best for you, and connected with your intuition, you won't be able to be present with your child and help your child to do the same. Susy fully embodies the notion that by turning within and healing ourselves, we, in turn, can heal our children.

Susy was able to make this journey about her self-healing, and the beautiful by-product of that is her relationship with both her daughter and her entire family healed. That's the way in.

The only way to heal a relationship with our children, partners, or families is first to heal ourselves. The carryover is so beautiful when those relationships begin to shift and change. As humans, we are not often gifted with the path; we might know a step or two, but we are generally merely walking through the storm with trust that we are going in the right direction.

Susy's book will give anyone who is struggling with themselves or their children a framework to begin this work. I want to commend Susy for piecing together the tools to begin her healing journey as it can sometimes be overwhelming. Incredibly, Susy has brought all the healing tools together in one place for mothers to take that first step on their journey.

Susy gives an empowering shift to parenting. She will provide you with a roadmap and guide to begin your self-healing journey but will also share the messiness and reality of parenting, which isn't perfect and shiny. It can be confronting and messy too, but that's ok. She shares her own stories and journey to help you understand you are not alone. You can have a childhood that is tainted and challenging, but with the right tools and support, you can heal on a deeper level and begin to cultivate an awakened life for yourself and your family.

Dr. Nicole LePera
Holistic Psychologist and Author

INTRODUCTION

This book has been whirling around my head for the last year. As I sit here on this almost cold, wintery morning in sunny Perth (the winters really aren't that bad in Australia), writing it feels like a scary process.

Will people read this book? Will mothers want to hear my words, and will my message penetrate deep into their souls and hearts? Can my words and story change lives? Will mothers find time to read this book? Will they give themselves the time?

Herein lies the problem, dear, beautiful reader. Honouring all that you are and giving yourself space to heal is what my message is ultimately about. You can only do the work if you give yourself time, that precious commodity we so readily ignore. How many times do you hear yourself say, *'I am so busy', 'I just don't have time', 'life is hectic',* or *'if I only I had more time'*? From a very early age, our children learn through observing our emotions. Can you look back and honestly remember a time when you had slow mornings and days spent in pyjamas with messy homes? Do you find yourself saying, 'today everything stops, and we will just be' or perhaps doing nothing for one hour or even a mere thirty minutes? We are now conditioned not only to run but to sprint through life. We are missing the small, precious moments that bring us back to love—love for ourselves and our children—and allowing ourselves to see comfort in the tiniest moments, whether gazing at the moon, watching our children play, watering the garden and seeing a rainbow through the water particles as the light hits them, having that extra cuddle in bed or warm socks and tea by the fire while reading a good book. The smallest of moments can give us so much pleasure, but they also force us to sit with the uncomfortableness of ourselves—and it's that which we run from the most.

As I write these words, I feel how beautiful it would be to allow ourselves to experience the wonders of life. I am going to be doing this work myself as I write because I need healing too. I need to slow down, I need to shed, and I need to give myself time and space. I need to allow myself to experience the wonder and light this incredible life gives us, instead of running through it like I'm in a race to win the title of fastest woman in the world. Imagine running a race like that and all you would do to gaze at the finish line—not look at the crowd or your competitors, but just keep your eyes straight ahead. Win the race. Run harder and faster, and keep your mind focused on winning. Can you see that so many of us are doing precisely that in life? We are striving for more, bigger, better, faster, and harder, yet we are missing out on the simplicity of life. We are not looking back or to the side; we are steamrolling ahead and missing the magic in the mundane.

If we stay busy, work harder, and run faster, we won't even need to sit in the silence and feel who we have become. In stillness, we will be able to see that this person, this woman isn't who we really are. I once read the words, 'We are all broken; that's how the light gets in', and now that resonates even more with my soul.

As you will discover in this book, my awakening came through my brokenness. I was at a time in my life where I felt like I truly hit rock bottom. Everyone's rock bottom is different. For some, it's money, for others, illness. Perhaps it's the death of a loved one, a relationship breakdown, or loss of a job. There can be so many different situations that can bring us to our lowest point. So many women have reached out to me over the last couple of years since I started to share my work profoundly and honestly, and began to show up as myself, not who society wanted me to be. I began to talk about the big stuff and the real things—the darkness, the brokenness—but I also guide people into their light. I believe we have inside of us the power to heal ourselves. We simply need someone to hold our hand for a while and walk with us on this new path. As we begin our journey, we start to believe in ourselves and to challenge everything we were taught about ourselves, life, and the world. We learn how to re-parent ourselves, and it is there that we start to come home to our true authentic selves. I believe true healing allows us to awaken to who we were meant to be in this life. We all had a soul contract when we entered this life, but conditioning, parenting, schooling, and other things that have happened to us have pushed most of us to forget what we are.

My awakening came through my eldest child—Seren, who was only six years old when she was diagnosed with ADHD, anxiety, and Oppositional Defiance Disorder. The journey shattered me into so many pieces that I forgot who I was. However, that unravelling became my awakening. When I started to put the parts of myself back together and healed, I saw myself for the first time—without conditioning, fear, lack, or the voices of self-doubt. Instead of seeing the ugly duckling in the lake, I saw the swan. My dream for you is that you become that beautiful white swan, glowing, healing, and rising into your authentic essence and power as a woman.

Only when we understand that we all have pain, sadness, and suffering, and when we allow ourselves to go to the hidden shadow parts of ourselves can we truly find home. For it is there that we make peace with ourselves, heal, and grow. From there, life softens. We stop running, and we stop being so busy that we even forget why we are so busy. We stop saying yes to everything to avoid the uncomfortableness of meeting our shadows. It is in the shadow space that we forgive and learn to let go of not only our brokenness and conditioning but also allow for ancestral imprinting to be released from our cells. We clear out the debris, and we fill in the dark holes with our light, and then magically, life becomes beautiful. I say all this because that was me; it was my journey—every single step.

For the last few years, I have been going through what I can only describe as a spiritual awakening. The process has not been all hearts and rainbows; the journey has been confronting, painful, deep, and more significant than I could have imagined. It has taken so many twists and turns and has gone into some dark spaces in my mind. I have had to go where I feared the most and open Pandora's box, but it was there that I found the golden ticket lying there waiting for me to open. Reflecting upon it now, I think, Woah, what a ride! I have lost friends and made new ones, and found my marriage at times overwhelming, but then slowly healed it, so my husband and I are now living deeply in love. The transformation only happened when I healed myself. I managed to see that my spirited child was here to awaken me. Her behaviour was the catalyst that broke me, but then allowed me to discover the shadows I had been running from for so long.

This book is written for you, my darling. Whether you have children already, are pregnant, or intend to be a mama in the future, this book will teach you how to heal from the inside out. It will give you a roadmap, so you aren't trying to navigate this journey alone. It is vital that as you begin your healing journey, you trust in the process. I will give you as much support and as many resources as I can through meditations, affirmations, prayers, mantras, and tools, such as future-self journalling. I use different words in the book, such as God, Universe, Spirit, and source. I have interchanged them to allow for diverse beliefs, but feel free to use a word of your choice that resonates with you. I also suggest purchasing a copy of my *Heal The Mother Journal*, as, throughout this book, I will be asking you to use the journal as you do the work.

The journal holds space for you to practise the powerful methods from this book and activate your healing through future-self journalling. The journal has been designed with loving illustrations crafted by an artist to complement the inspiring mantras and give visual cues to boost your healing practise. Using the journal and my guidance from this book together, you will begin to let go of fear, self-ridicule, anxiety, regret, and instead, help you to meet yourself with love and acceptance.

I have included many more mantras and affirmations for you, which I have infused throughout the book. If you find one that resonates with your soul, it will help you to activate the light within. Pop the message on a Post-It® note and place it on your bathroom mirror, so that you may see it each day.

This book isn't about diets, supplements, green smoothies, or kale chips (although I am quite partial to them). Instead, this book is about you beginning your healing from the grassroots. We have been able to self-heal since the beginning of time, but these teachings have been suppressed or stolen. Women have been hunted as witches and were stopped from healing each other. Women have been gifted with the ability to create life, yet even that has become something to be feared. There is so much fear ingrained in each cell of female bodies that we have forgotten within us lies the ability to heal not only ourselves but our children and future generations.

So, I ask you, dear one, are you ready? Are you ready to heal? Take a deep breath in, close your eyes, place your hand on your heart, and breathe in and out slowly. Allow your shoulders to soften, find your smile from within, and let's do this together—let's heal.

CHAPTER 1

YOUR UNRAVELLING MAY SIMPLY
BE YOUR REBIRTH.

I remember it like it was yesterday. I was curled up in the foetal position, rocking and crying uncontrollably. However, I wasn't falling apart. I was crawling into my cocoon, now ready and willing to feel the pain and begin my metamorphosis. Once I learned the truth—pain always comes before the rising—I was able to let go of the dark binds that I set upon myself and surrender to all that needed to be healed.

When I look back on my mental health breakdown that happened five years ago, I am now able to see clearly that, in fact, it was my breakthrough. At the time, I didn't have the tools, and I was drowning—not slowly, but fully pelting into the darkness of the abyss. There was no gentle awakening; it was full throttle descent into brokenness.

However, my awakening was where I first discovered the concept of 'heal the mother, heal the child'. In my last book, *The Diary of an ADHD Mum*, I shared our story of learning to live, love, and laugh while parenting a child with ADHD.

ves insight into the home and heart of a mother
fe with a different type of child. As a family, we
ADHD as a trait, merely a different way to be. We
have ster 1 out of the old paradigm that ADHD is a disorder,
and we now only choose to see it as just a different way to be.

Before I got to this space, I was immersed in self-doubt,
self-loathing, and a victimhood mentality. I didn't believe in
myself as a mother. The story I was telling myself prevented
me from stepping into my power and supporting my daughter
through love instead of scarcity and fear. Back then, I couldn't
see it. I was drowning in anxiety, overwhelm, and probably
undiagnosed post-natal depression (PND), and I was falling
further and further down the rabbit hole!

We emigrated to Perth, Australia, when my youngest son
Flynn was only four months old, my other daughter Daisy
was two, and Seren was six. When I look back now, I wonder
whether I had PND brought on by such a big move. Even
though we had been planning the move for two years, nothing can prepare you for the shock of leaving your family and
closest friends, especially when you are still in the postpartum
phase. I felt the separation and isolation as soon as our feet
touched down on Australian soil. It wasn't that long ago that
women were in tribes, raising their babies together along with
their elders. To think how separate we have now become, often
raising our children alone I am sure is affecting us more than
we realise.

The HypnoBirthing Years

Years ago, when I was a HypnoBirthing practitioner, I would
teach women about the history of birthing. I would share
with women that pregnancy and birth was a sacred time for
women. I would explain that long ago, humans didn't understand the correlation between sex and conception. Women were
almost worshipped as it seemed they could have babies at will.
There were temples, shrines, and statues of pregnant women,
and the men would worship them. When the woman would

begin to labour, the other women in the village would take the women into the cave, often in a stream or running water, and the men would wait outside. The birthing woman was loved upon, supported, and celebrated. How different when we look at the birthing industry now and see how fear is completely running the show.

Women are led to believe their bodies aren't capable of a natural, drug-free birth. When fear is present, your adrenal glands send catecholamines into your blood. The catechol-amines block the endorphins from flowing into the body, and therefore the birthing mothers feel only pain. We stop the natural flow of ease and grace when we choose fear over love. We mask the beautiful effects of the natural production of morphine that is produced for this time in our life. The body is way more complex and sophisticated than we give it credit for. Our body in the right environment has the power to heal and support itself.

When I look back now, I see that Seren's behaviour became so out of control when we moved to Australia, as she was mirroring me. My emotions—fear, anxiety, and panic—about moving here were playing out through her. Often children reflect the emotions and behaviour of their mothers and the people closest to them, and that is why this healing work is so important. If we have issues with our children, we must heal ourselves first.

My husband, Karl, decided at the time of our move that he wanted to 'find himself'. I look back now and smile, but at the time, it was difficult. He had worked incredibly hard over the previous decade to grow a business and then sell it. It took time to adjust. He felt lost as his life became helping me change nappies and burp babies. That wasn't his world; it was mine, and he struggled with the transition. To cope, he travelled quite a lot, and I found myself feeling even more isolated and alone.

I had my last two babies at home in a birthing pool in Wales. We grew vegetables, had chickens, and lived a simple life in the country. I had dreamt of moving to Australia for so long, but I always look back and think, *what was the rush?* Life was so hectic that I honestly can't remember Flynn's early months of life. As soon as we set foot in Australia, Seren's behaviour was so bad that our life became constant meetings and appointments with teachers and experts.

The chaos went on for about twelve months, and through that time, we started trial medication for Seren. As a mum who tried so hard to have natural births, minimal vaccinations, and grow vegetables without chemicals, I found the process so very difficult. I honestly feel that is why my mental health deteriorated so much. I was out of alignment with my beliefs and values, and I completely lost myself.

Seeking Help

My aha moment came when I found myself in the doctor's surgery shortly after we emigrated to Australia, begging him for antidepressants. I felt so isolated, anxious, and lost that I couldn't even think clearly. I had never done anything like this before, yet here I was, desperate and in need of help with my mental health.

My doctor believed I wasn't genuinely depressed, and it was merely a symptom of my life. He said, 'Susy, you aren't depressed. You are just far away from your family and friends and struggling to know what to do for your child'.

Gosh, I don't know if ever more accurate words were spoken! I got it, and I understood what he was saying. However, I had no idea how to fix my feelings, and it was affecting my relationship with my husband and my children. I was continually living in the fight or flight mode and reacting to everything with fear. My body was continuously flooded with cortisol. That is not how we are designed to work, and that way of life is not sustainable. I was moving headfirst into a huge crash without a safety harness!

I cried from morning until night. I hated myself, and I didn't want to leave the house. I had no interest in sex or a connection with Karl, and I was even considering my existence. My doctor suggested talking to the naturopath and supporting my mental health naturally (seriously, what a guy), but I felt like I didn't have a stable foundation, and the bricks to my house were crashing down. I had no idea which way to turn or how to begin healing and helping myself, so I convinced the doctor to give me pills!

The antidepressants kicked in straight away. I felt a completely natural high and like I should be heading to the nightclub, not the school run. I felt everything more intensely, and I felt at peace, calm, and happy. It was instant. It's important to note that this is just my story. My doctor confirmed that I wasn't genuinely depressed, and that is why the medication worked so quickly.

Once I started on the medication, which was only half the recommended dose, I began to see clearly. I could step out of the hazy darkness that had been plaguing me for the last few months, and I started to drag myself back up from the gutter of my thoughts. The children's screams, fights, and demands suddenly paled into insignificance. Seren's crazy and outlandish behaviour didn't trigger me, and life suddenly felt a whole lot happier. On the flip side, I was unable to cry (seriously, not even one tear) and was unable to orgasm! It made me realise how powerful these drugs were. Yes, my situation now was a lot easier to manage. My husband loved the 'new me' and supported me as having made the right decision but taking away two of my greatest loves—this was mean! Women release a lot through both tears and orgasms; this is how we are programmed.

> In the absence of fear, we walk the true path of our existence.

Shame Around Sex

I want to share here briefly something I have learned over the last few months. It's called sacred sexuality. I discovered that in the Western World, we don't fully embrace sexual pleasure or even how supportive orgasms can be when it comes to menstrual cramps. Our bodies are built for so much magic, but due to shame around sexual pleasure, this knowledge is often shunned. We have been raised to avoid the subject of sex, not fully understanding or celebrating it. Sex can also be looked upon as something to feel shameful about. I even felt guilt telling my dad I was pregnant with Seren—at the age of 29. I was married to Karl, and we had been together for six years, yet the guilt and shame that came up for me when I told my dad made me feel so embarrassed.

The last time I saw my birth mother was when I was pregnant with Seren. She couldn't even look at me and found it so difficult to accept that I was pregnant. I will never understand why she acted that way or why so much shame came up for her. What I do know is that it was her shame coming up and it had nothing to do with me. Pregnancy and birth are two of the greatest wonders of the world, and women should always be made to feel proud, loved, and supported during those life phases.

That is part of the problem with the Western World. We don't celebrate women, birth, or even the act of making love; we shun it and don't fully embrace it. It is part of the disconnection between women and men. We aren't taught to embody all aspects of the sacred self fully. It is time we begin to change the old paradigm and pull forth all the ancient wisdoms that were buried and hidden many moons ago.

When we orgasm, our bodies release hormones such as oxytocin and DHEA. These hormones are extremely relaxing for women and have many health benefits that can protect us from heart disease and cancer. Oxytocin is the so-called love hormone which is also produced when we give birth. This rush of oxytocin gives women the intense love for our babies as soon as they are born. There is a reason for this potent magic and to take a drug that took these hormones away just didn't seem right to me. When we cry, we also release oxytocin. Again, our body is always trying to bring us back to a homeostatic state, but are we working with it or against it? Are we allowing our systems to be fuelled by fear or fuelled by love?

Crying Is Letting Go

I once read that we must allow our children to cry, as when they cry it lets the hurt out. We shouldn't shout at them and tell them to 'toughen up', and we shouldn't try and encourage them with love to stop crying. Instead, we should support them to let it out and hold space for them. I believe that is why children cry so much; they don't shame themselves, they have no agenda, and their ego isn't loud enough yet. They show us the way—it is good to cry, and we need it. We release trauma, pain, and sadness out of our bodies instead of allowing it to bury itself deep within. I knew that the two necessary parts of myself that my incredible body had the power to release—trauma and joy—were being suppressed and could not be the answer long term. However, at the time, I didn't have another healing path, so the medication gave me a quick fix. It gave me room to breathe for a while. I was happy, my little family was happy, and life seemed a lot rosier!

Now, here's the thing; here is my aha moment. Almost overnight, Seren's behaviour changed. The hyperactivity, defiance, and impulsivity changed in an instant. Karl noticed and commented on how maybe she had been copying my behaviour? That was the first time I started to understand the actual connection between mother and child. I think we feel that connection only happens with babies, but I have learned that a child has that connection with their mother until around the age of eight years old, maybe even longer. Children are so intrinsically linked to us and our mental health can affect them more than we know. As a mama with a spirited child, I have learned that Seren—even at the age of almost thirteen—is still linked to my emotions far more than my other two children, Daisy and Flynn. They always have been the same, and rarely do my feelings trigger them.

Our Campervan Travels

As I write this chapter, we are travelling around Australia for two months in a campervan. I didn't book the trip until the last minute, and I couldn't work out why. Something had blocked me from booking it. Part of the reason for writing this book is to guide women back to their intuition and help them learn to trust it. I will be talking about that more in this book, but two parts of ourselves steer our ship through life. One is the journey of the heart which always brings us back to love and connects us with our higher selves. The other is our ego which is the part of ourselves that tries to keep us safe and lives out of fear. Most of our programming was set in childhood and can often be driven by conditioning fear and ridicule. That is not the true essence of our higher self, and when we let our ego run the show, it takes us along a path that is tainted with confusion and self-doubt. This book will help you learn to know how to break fear from your ego, and instead, connect only to the purest part of ourselves. In essence, healing is freedom. It will allow us not only to reparent ourselves but not to pass down the old paradigm to our children. We can find a new way to parent our children, based on love, not fear.

Listening in to my intuition, I tried to understand why I still hadn't booked our trip even though we were leaving in a mere six weeks. One day while sitting with Seren, I turned to her and asked, 'Are you excited about the road trip honey'?

'No', she replied. 'I don't want to go. I don't want to travel with Daisy and Flynn. They annoy me, and I don't want to go'.

And there it was. My intuition had been trying to guide me not to book this trip as I had known something wasn't right. I hadn't rushed into booking it as I trusted in the universe. I believe in the divine timing of everything and trust that everything happens precisely when it's supposed to. I have a deep knowing and belief that we are always being guided, and when we trust, our path will become clear. It's not always easy to do, but the more I practise, the easier it becomes.

As we continued chatting, I joked with Seren. 'What are we going to do then? Send you to the UK'?

Seren jumped and screamed with delight. 'Mum, please, yes, this is what I want so much. I don't want to go on the trip with you. I want to go and see my family and friends'.

Parenting A Wild One

One of the lessons that I have learned from parenting a spirited child is that they have a mission here on this earth. For Seren, she is not interested in travelling around and being free for seven weeks, and she is not excited about the beach, nature, and being in the moment; this kid has shit to do. She has always been that way. Daisy and Flynn will spend hours playing make-believe games, but that has never, ever interested Seren. In Bali, when Daisy and Flynn wanted to swim for hours, Seren would instead scour the streets looking for sick dogs and helping them. We all love going to the farmer's market on a Saturday. However, for Seren, she prefers to go and see a homeless man called Damian just outside the market. Seren takes food and drinks for him and spends her pocket money to buy him warm clothes from the charity shop. She is wired differently, and she has purpose and meaning in this life that goes far beyond 'playing the perfect happy family'. She sees flaws in the system and wants to fix it. She is an indigo child for sure, and now I trust everything she brings forth to me in this life, even though it's often hard parenting her.

When she told me that she wanted to go to the UK for three weeks, there was never any doubt in my mind that is what she needed. Selfishly, I realised we all needed it. I feel we all needed a break and honouring that and allowing anxiety and ego to step aside was a big thing for me. If my ego and fear were running the show, there was no way I would let my twelve-year-old travel to the UK for three weeks without us, but my heart and my intuition told me that was what we needed.

It was during this time away from Seren that I was able to rest for a while. I was always immersed in the work, allowing the triggers to guide me, trying to come back to love, and going within and trying to find the lesson within the challenges. During that time, I was able to relax and not be triggered so deeply every day. If you are a mother with a spirited child, try and get as much time for yourself as you can. You need to have moments when you allow yourself to breathe, reset, and focus on you, instead of always focusing on your child. If you can, take help from family and friends, or encourage your partner to help you out, as giving yourself space and time is often the tonic you need. If you don't have support from family or the child's father, then maybe reach out to your village. School mums, friends; we all need our community to raise our children. Do not be scared to ask for help!

> We can either feel the pain now, awaken to it, heal it, and live a conscious life, or we stay asleep, and our children will have to deal with the pain later.

Gratitude for My Spirited Child

The one thing I took from Seren being away from us is how different my life would have been without a spirited child. Her behaviour has brought up so much inside me that for the last two years, both Karl and I have been healing deep, unhealed wounds from our childhoods. I truly believe that without Seren I would still be living in *The Truman Show*-style, going through life oblivious and existing in a manmade and false matrix of evolution.

Like the fake world of social media and all the accounts we follow to make us feel good, when, in fact, all they do is make us feel unworthy and a failure. Instagram is not real life. When we see it for what it is, we can lessen the grip and addiction it has on us. Don't get me wrong—some accounts have changed my life profoundly and positively, but many don't and that can make me feel like a failure. Check-in with yourself, lean into how some accounts make you feel and maybe consider taking some time to have a social media detox for as long as possible.

These are only my suggestions—sink into your intuition and do what feels right to you. The only reason I was able to write this book was to come off social media. The addiction was real, and I know so many feel this way. What did you love doing that you have now replaced with social media? Writing, knitting, baking, playing board games or reading; what in your life has been replaced by scrolling? Sit what that for a minute and ask your heart; do I need a social media detox?

Another thing I have discovered is that there is an epidemic of anxiety in children and in mothers. I am still so alarmed that the medical model is not supporting and helping mothers and instead is diagnosing and medicating children. If we want to heal our children, we must go first—the healing must begin with us. If we put into the mix epigenetics, ancestral trauma, and the chemical soup that our children are born into, it's no wonder that so many of our children are struggling. Yet here is the thing—they are also our biggest teachers. They have chosen us to be their mothers, as they have something in this life to teach us. They are the gatekeepers to our wounds if we allow the triggers to take us there. The key to their healing is that it starts with you. It can be messy, confronting, and challenging, yet beautiful and life-changing. It is important work, and my book will lovingly carry you, support you, and hold space for your healing.

My Child Was My Mirror

After I began medication for my mental health, I went back to see my doctor weeks later so he could assess how I'd been feeling after taking the medication. He was an excellent and cautious medicating doctor (which is so rare these days), and he only prescribed me one month of antidepressants. I told him the dramatic effect my medication had on Seren. I urged that if mothers came to him complaining of their child and worrying that they had anxiety and ADHD, he should work on fixing the mama first. He laughed, but I emphasized to him that seriously it was no joke; it was a miracle.

At the time, I still didn't understand this work and what it meant. It was years later while deep in the thick of my healing journey that I came across the work of the incredible, late Louise Hay. She was the first person who talked about mirroring and how another person close to us can project out to the world the very thing that we don't like about ourselves. Very recently, I have come to learn that this also applies to the people we admire. The qualities we love and respect in them are also how we portray ourselves to the world. We are all one, we are all connected, and I will be delving deep into this subject and sharing with you my experience with that interconnectedness.

Last year I went to Bali on a week-long breath facilitators course. This work with thirteen other women was deep, confronting, emotional, and at times, scary, as we delved into the parts of our unconsciousness that we try and keep suppressed. I felt like I removed my mask for the first time and uncovered parts of myself I'd tried to hide my entire life. Those parts of ourselves that lie dormant, so instead we live a life that isn't genuinely congruent with our soul's purpose—we have forgotten who we are.

Finding Our Light

We allow these parts of ourselves to sit there rotting away, hoping that one day they will pass. Little do we realise that these shadows stop us from being our authentic selves. They keep us small, afraid, weak, and at times self-loathing. We feel anxious, worried, self-judging, self-doubting, and a million other emotions that don't truly reflect our inner magnificence and beauty to the world. To uncover and release these parts of ourselves is truly removing the mask and starting to heal and to live authentically.

What has been so fascinating for me is the outpouring of messages online I received from mothers sharing their journeys. Many of them would tell me that their children were not broken, they had no issues in school or at home, but as women that felt like they were drowning. They would tell me how they didn't enjoy their jobs anymore and felt so pulled towards doing something else. Their lives ticked all the boxes— beautiful house, husband, kids, good job, friends, etc.—but they felt something was missing. They had started to question everything around them.

They started to look at their children and realise how much they didn't want the same for them. Some women had been sufferers of different types of abuse either in childhood or later in life. As women have done for decades, they had just buried the trauma, put on a brave face, and began to forget all the pain.

Most of us unintentionally and unconsciously bring our children into this world. We haven't been taught to do the work, release the trauma, heal what needs healing, and detox our bodies—physically, spiritually, and emotionally—before we conceive. Therefore, we can unintentionally pass these unhealed and unprocessed traumas onto the baby.

We can repeat all the patterns, just as our parents did, and this is where the term 'generational trauma' fits in. We are unknowingly passing down the ancestral line pain, suffering and patterns. One of the most exciting things about this time in history is that we are finally learning to heal, let go, and move generational trauma through our bodies. Through this art, we can consciously stop the generational trauma and change our future lineage. What a privilege!

To Feel Is to Heal

We haven't been taught how to feel. Just keep going, fit in, keep up with the Joneses, that is why so many of us are anxious, depressed, and unhappy. We see the world, and we feel the pain, so we numb it with alcohol, sex, work, social media, and illicit or pharmaceutical drugs. Who is really winning here and who is losing? From the outside looking in, it certainly isn't us, but the tides are turning. We see the conditioning, we see the BS, and we want change. We demand change. Furthermore, we deserve change, and so do our future generations.

Throughout this book, I will be sharing the stories of other men and women. If we are to heal and evolve, we need to feel into all those other stories. If we think back to how the village used to be, it was such a connection of souls. We would hear about the women in the red tent, who during the new moon would all gather with their children and babies and menstruate together. It's no accident that women menstruate together. We are deeply connected—much more than we realise. Some people believe that when we menstruate the veil to the spirit world is thinner, and we can get more in-depth divine wisdom and feel more deeply. We have been conditioned that pre-menstrual feelings are negative, and we can become irritated with our partners, work colleagues, children, and friends, but we haven't been taught how to harness that wisdom and power and feel into all that it brings us. I believe that even anxiety around this time has something to teach us, and we will explore that in more depth later in this book.

> I started to ask my anxiety, What do you have to teach me?

Flowing with My Menstruation

Have you ever considered that during our menstruation, or our moon time as I like to call it, we need to slow down, go inwards, work on ourselves, love on ourselves, and allow our intuition to show us the truth? We haven't been taught to look at this as a sacred flow and a time when our energy shifts—a potent time when we should be slowing down and going within. We have truly lost touch with our spiritual selves, and that has brought us to the place in time where we are anxious, depressed, and angry. We have lost touch with the essence of who we are. It's like we have hit the wall. In the movie *The Truman Show*, Jim Carrey tries to escape from his 'fake and meaningless life' in a boat and then hits the wall. He realised his whole life was only a television show, and he was simply living a fake existence.

So many of us have hit that wall, so to speak, and it is here that we find the crossroads. Numb our pain or bravely take steps to get out of the boat and, just like Jim Carrey, climb those steps, open the door and walk into a new version of ourselves. How funny it is now that in 'real-life' Jim Carrey has truly awakened and talks of these shifts in the media. It's rather sad that the media has somehow tried to make out that Jim has gone slightly mad, yet he says he feels more alive than ever, channelling his gifts through his painting and artwork.

It's important to mention here that some of the most awakened gurus of our time—living in India—seemed to go 'insane' as they awakened. If they had been living in the Western World, they would have been locked up and deemed crazy, but in India, they were respected, trusted, and allowed to awaken. Just remember that when you feel like you are going mad on this journey!

I have been lucky that over the last few years my friendships have shifted, and the women and men around me are awakened too. During some of the most insane times, which I will share in this book, without their love and support, I would have felt like I was going crazy. But through their guidance and support, they lovingly reminded me that I was simply awakening to my gifts. I was beginning to remember who I was without fear and conditioning. My friends and Karl all held space for me listened to me and loved on me, and this gave me room to grow even further. That is my intention for you—that you know you are truly loved, supported, and divinely guided as you go along this path.

I Am Healing Too

I also want to share with you how important this book is for me. When I started to write it, I was in a great place. My work and my message were getting out to mainstream media. My online community was connecting with me more than ever, my husband was going through a spiritual awakening, and my kids were great. Life felt amazing! I was deep in the work. Healing, breathwork, meditation, journalling—this all felt amazing! After everything I had been through in my life, my issues with ADHD and premenstrual dysphoric disorder or PMDD, which I will share with you in more depth later, my struggles with my daughter, and some of my mental health issues, this phase was beautiful. I felt deeply connected to my kids, to Karl, and the world around me.

I was writing this book, re-publishing my other book, holding full moon circles and breathwork circles, and managing an Airbnb business. I was working on shedding some pounds, exercising, and was going through an incredible awakening of discovering some medium gifts. There is never a dull moment, and I will get this to that later.

Even writing this now, I can see the problem; I was on the never-ending treadmill. We have been conditioned and brainwashed that to create success, we must be like the hamster on the wheel!

There was no time for my spiritual practise and daily self-care. I was not slowing down, not meditating, not using any of the tools that had previously helped me. I was using essential oils, but that was pretty much it. Guess what happened?

Yup, I had a full-on breakdown.

My mental health plummeted. I cried a lot. I became distant with Karl; our bond and connection became non-existent. I started shouting at the kids (for being kids). I couldn't cope with their arguing and meltdowns, and then finally it happened. My beautiful daughter once again became my mirror.

Our Children Can Reflect Our Pain

I watched my eldest daughter have a full-on breakdown over a pair of trousers (that I accidentally ever-so-slightly shrunk in the dryer). She wailed like a baby, she screamed and shouted, she slammed doors, even started swearing, fuck this, shit that—it was horrible to watch. It went on for 30 mins, and I had no idea how to stop the tsunami of emotion. I witnessed her little brain and body contort and squirm in overdrive. She had no idea how to stop it, and I left her to work through it. I knew it would be a day we were late for school! The morning was horrendous, but it was also another big awakening for me. Seren was simply mirroring me. I had not been working on myself. I had pain in both of my shoulders, it was hard to sleep, my lower back ached, and I felt numb. Despite my preaching of healing and self-care to other mums, I had done none of it for the last four weeks. I had only piled more and more onto my shoulders (literally).

My boundaries were shot. I was taking on more and more, I was worried about offending people, and I was giving a lot through social media and not doing anything for myself. Karl was working so much more, but he was also doing so much for his mental health—meeting a group of people every morning at 5 am and swimming in the ocean and doing breathwork and meditation on the beach five days a week. I was happy for him, I really was, but also annoyed at myself for doing absolutely nothing. However, everything happens for a reason. People say that when you write a book, you should write it for yourself; it can be so cathartic, and when we heal ourselves, in turn, we heal others.

So, as you do this work, know that I have been doing it with you and will continue to do so. Collectively, we all are beginning to heal across the world. We are going through a mass awakening at a rate that the world has never seen before. This work and your healing journey will have a ripple effect for future generations to come—never underestimate the power of taking those few tiny steps.

Mental Health Epidemic

I remember watching an interview with Eckhart Tolle during which he was asked, 'Why are we going through such a huge mental health epidemic'? His answer astounded me and gave me hope. He talked about the Bible and how it spoke of a re-birth. He shared how, at first, we must go through the pain before we can go through the resurrection and be re-born. If we think for a moment about what Jesus went through—first the pain, then the rising—that is how it works, what is needed, and the reason we have come to earth. We have come here to learn and to ascend. Each lifetime is necessary for the understanding and lessons; we have not come here only for the magic. That is only in the fairy tales. Knowing that pain and suffering is part of the re-birth can be so freeing. We stop trying to find paradise and searching for happiness and instead trust the journey and all its lessons. We can find peace in the smallest of moments as we stop searching. We come to learn that all we have is the present moment, and we begin to find joy from that. It is why we came here, and once we understand that, we can truly discover that heaven can be here on earth.

Eckhart shared how women in childbirth will get to the point when they feel they can't go on; the midwife knows those signs and trusts that birth is only moments away. We must go to that point, to surrender to it fully, and to embody the pain as it means that the new life is imminent. First, the shock, then new life—re-birth. Do you see what Eckhart is trying to teach us? We are going through a mass awakening, and part of that can be pain and suffering, but on the other side is a victory as your higher self calls you forward. If you are in that place right now, I want you to trust it. I want you to honour these feelings and trust that your re-birth is coming, my friend.

To help you with this part, I want you to begin with future-self journalling and I have included a full guide on how to begin this practice in Chapter 10. We aren't going to sit with these feelings and go over and over them and allow them to keep us in this loop of suffering and confusion. We are going to begin walking the path to rising. My suggestions for you are to find a breathwork class, such as shamanic, holotropic, or conscious connected breathwork. I have included some links in Chapter 10, as breathwork for me has been one of the quickest ways to help bring all the trauma to the surface and release it out of my body. If you have some deep-rooted fears, or something

On the other side of your awakening is the path to your gifts and your reason for your incarnation on earth. But first, you must open Pandora's box as it is there you will find the key to your life.

is holding you back, I would also try something called Psych-K. After two sessions, I was able to get over the two of my biggest fears—freeway driving and public speaking. I cannot recommend this practise enough. It truly has been life-changing for me.

The Generational Curse

As we close this chapter, I feel it's important to share a bit about my upbringing and how our mothers can affect us. It's also so important that we don't blame our parents. I believe we chose them for a reason, as there were things we needed to learn in this life. The burden then lies with us, not them. I firmly believe that our parents didn't have the tools to do the work. They were parenting us as they had been parented themselves. If we consider our grandparents and great-grandparents, they were in survival mode and trying to cope during wars or maybe even conflicts. They didn't have access to mobile phones, the internet, and even their food was rationed. When they said goodbye to their husbands who went to war, they had no idea if they would ever see them again. They had no way of contacting them for long periods and had to cope in a scary world trying as best they could. Can you even imagine that for a second? They were in survival mode and living in the fight or flight mode. I always remember my mother telling me that when her father returned from the war, she would at times find him with his head in the gas oven. He was severely traumatised, but at the time, they didn't understand about PTSD, so there was little support, compassion, or understanding.

If we go further back to our ancestors, we know that they experienced war, famine, and severe trauma. Now, through epigenetics, we understand the link created between the mother during conception and the child. As I shared in *The Diary of an ADHD Mum*, when Seren was conceived and born, she had way too much cortisol in her system. When I conceived Seren, I'd had one the craziest twelve months ever! Even when I look back now, I see that my breakdown was trying to lead me to my awakening. However, little I did I know that an awakening can come in the disguise of a breakdown. I didn't understand that everything I was going through would lead me to heal and awaken to the truth of who I am. And to think my daughter was part of this. I used to hold such guilt about it, but I now see she chose me for a reason, and we both came into this world to help each other. A friend told me yesterday that her spirited son chose their family for a reason. Even though at four years old he's super challenging, she understands that he needed to come to their family so he could be accepted and loved. I have always felt the same with Seren.

The Universe Was Knocking on My door

I feel like the Universe was trying to knock on the door so many times, yet I kept on missing the signs. I had a lot of mental health issues around the age of 28 that seemed to come out of nowhere, but I feel that my whole life was bringing me to this point. I was living in London, but it was so difficult for me, as I was a country girl and not a city girl. I was caught up in the London bombs shortly after arriving, and that started the beginning of my travelling anxiety. Throw into the mix a big operation, a car crash, a huge move away from family and friends, a house renovation, living away from Karl, a new job, and a wedding all in twelve months, and it's no wonder I started to have anxiety and panic attacks. When I look back at that time, I see that my spirit was sending me to this point to awaken. Shortly after we got married, I was pregnant, and my focus became this amazing new life inside me. I wish I knew back then the importance of healing myself before I got pregnant. I wish I'd been taught that we must heal our bodies before we have a baby and that all our toxins, emotions, unhealed pain, and trauma and childhood issues would be woven into that little foetus. No one tells you that. For me, that is one of the most important things that we should ever be taught.

Through epigenetics, scientists have also discovered that the way the father feels before conception can also affect the baby. It is so important that we take the path of healing before trying for a baby—the healing of emotions, not just the body. It's also vital that you do not blame yourself if, like me, you didn't know this before you conceived your child. I trust that Seren chose me to be her mama. She knew we had work to do in this life, and I am forever grateful that she chose me, as I know it is my life's purpose to teach this work.

I genuinely believe you need to go through the work to teach and inspire others, and without Seren and all the issues that we endured, I would never have discovered my gift of writing and wanting to help others rise even through discomfort. I want to teach mothers that it's ok if your child isn't perfect, and you feel like you are failing. There is a reason for all that is happening to you and your child—holding trust in your heart is the biggest gift you can give yourself and your child.

If it hadn't been for my daughter and my challenging childhood, I would have been locked in *The Truman Show* way of life, existing and looking shiny and together on the outside but slowly suffocating on the inside. For her, I am forever grateful.

You Are Braver Than You Think

As we begin this work together, I want you to honour yourself for being brave enough to do it. Have full confidence in yourself that this is your time and know what this work is for—this book chose you!

Never allow the guilt of past mistakes to cloud your thinking about your magnificence. Within you is a light that is dying to shine out to the world. Releasing all guilt of the past will ensure your light isn't dimmed. Maya Angelou once said, 'Do the best you can until you know better. Then when you know better, do better.' Hold this in your heart and never look back.

When I think back to the time that I was conceived, I can only imagine the trauma and suffering that surrounded my mother. She had never gotten over the death of her father. In some ways, I feel she carried some sort of guilt, but I can't work out what. She loved him dearly. Although I never met him, she told me how she was like his shadow and went everywhere with him. She always referred to him as 'Daddy' and said he was one of the kindest men she had ever met. I feel she longed for that in her marriages, but after two failed—one of them to my dad—she still wanted that type of love.

She was never close to her mother, and yet from what she told me she was a good daughter. My nana never approved of her. It's funny; I feel she played this role with me, too, from a very young age. I remember being closer to my nana than I was with my mother. My mother was someone who attracted drama and chaos into her life, so just like Seren, maybe I was conceived with too much cortisol? My dad also had some mental health issues, which began when he was a young adult. He was a highly successful bank manager in his early twenties, but for almost fifteen years, he didn't sleep for more than three hours per night. He became obsessed with worrying about his death and couldn't sleep. He told me that miraculously it just stopped and he didn't understand how it started or even more so, how it ended so suddenly. He was so successful and driven in so many areas of his life, but I can't imagine how hard it was for him to exist on only three hours of sleep per night for all those years. I remember my dad telling me he said one day to my mum, 'Gosh, look at us both. How on earth will Susy turn out'?

I have to say, I have had the most incredible life, and I am so grateful for all the lessons, but jeez it been hard trying to navigate this life without a roadmap. I had a very challenging and complex childhood, and I began to rebel a lot in my teens, but I worked hard and always believed in fairy tales. Thankfully my fairy tale came true; I am one of the lucky ones, and I will forever have so much gratitude for how my life has turned out.

Ultimately, as I have mentioned, we choose our parents. I know that I chose mine as I had lessons to learn in this life-time. I am grateful for all the lessons, suffering, journey, and mistakes. Not having a relationship with my mother has been hard, but on the flip side, it has made me a passionate, loving mother. I try hard to be the mother I craved, and for this, I am eternally grateful.

Along the way, and again through epigenetics, I have learned that a lot of what I was feeling wasn't even my stuff; it was my mum's. Fears, anxieties, and her emotional turmoil were projected into me. I discovered that a lot of my pain wasn't mine, but simply passed down the ancestral line. However, it is possible to rid yourself of that pain and learn to release it from your cells and your spirit. I have done this, so I know it is possible. Through future-self journalling, breathwork, meditation and other healing modalities, it is possible to release and let go. Once we learn to shed and let go, we can be who we were meant to be in this life. That is my dream for you as we walk through this book together and do the work.

CHAPTER 2
THE DARK NIGHT OF THE SOUL.

I stayed up most of the night tossing and turning and feeling a tightness in my chest. Curled up on the sofa with my dog, I watched the clouds go past in the sky, illuminated by the moon and eerily turning into scary faces and monsters. It was one of the longest and strangest nights of my life as my brain tried to process what was happening, but it was from this point that my awakening began to take many different forms. It needed to begin this way for the magic to unfold.

Everyone's awakening is different, but what seems to be commonplace is that the awakening can begin from a place of darkness. A place we can get to in our lives through sickness, addiction, divorce, trauma, death, or another event that shocks us to the core can catapult us into an awakening. I have seen many of my friends awaken over the last few years, and I truly believe who you are as a person affects the outcome of the awakening. However, an awakening can also come from being completely out of alignment from our true selves.

I remember years ago when we first moved to Australia. I was so far out of alignment with my true self that it caused massive issues with my mental health and self-esteem. Both Karl and I worked hard together to build a dream of ours—to sell Karl's business and move to Australia. I had focused so much on that goal, and everything was based on the result. I even manifested to conceive my beautiful boy Flynn twelve months before we emigrated. Everything was based on that move, but when we arrived, things took a turn for the worse.

I started to attract people and situations into my life that weren't congruent with my beliefs and my values. The more I did that, the more I drifted away from my true self, but at this point, I didn't know who my true self was, I was so lost in the abyss. I was homesick, lonely, and lost in a world of fear as my eldest daughter was diagnosed with ADHD and anxiety. My mental health deteriorated, and I felt like such a failure. I suffered from anxiety and overwhelming sadness.

No Support Network

I didn't have the people, support, or tools around me to help me lovingly see that I was at the beginning of awakening. So instead, I decided to go to the doctor and ask for help. I did get help from the doctor, and I am truly grateful. Taking medication for five months helped me so much. It allowed me to see once again without the heavy cloud following me around, but in many ways, it prevented me from awakening. However, my awakening was waiting for me. As soon as I came off the medication, all those original feelings were still there, but by that time, I was ready!

Everything happens as it should, nothing is an accident, and we should learn to trust in the divine timing of life. One of my dear friends told me that she started to awaken as a teenager and was always known as the hippie one. She also vowed to take her awakening slowly and has pretty much continued this pace her whole life. I was also starting to see some of my other friends awaken as they began to learn the truth about vaccines, government, veganism, etc., and slowly they began to ask questions, seek alternatives, and dip their toes into a new way of being.

Others have told me how they started to see the beauty in things and that nature blooming in the summer would move them to such tears that they would have to pull the car over to compose themselves. I have other friends who are now starting to awaken as they begin their path with healing modalities, such as reiki and breathwork. That excites me so much, as I can see how things are going to change for them, and it's a beautiful thing. I am having more open conversations with people now about the universe, source energy, spiritual guides and God, and this fills my heart, as people are beginning to wake up from the deepest sleep.

I have experienced all these things, but I experienced a rude awakening which I was not expecting. In a world that doesn't openly talk about spiritual awakenings, I felt alone, and at times, scared. I decided to begin my awakening—as I do with most things in my life—at one million miles an hour. My life at the time was planned with complete precision. However, over the last twelve months, I have learned to slow down, trust the process, and let the universe surprise me, and I love this new version of myself.

My Awakening

My awakening came in my search for belonging. My entire life from the age of fifteen has been a series of moves to new houses and places, and even countries. I also read the quote the other day that 'Not all who wander are lost'; however, it certainly didn't apply to me. I was so lost and was continually searching for the place that would feel like home, which I have come to realise is merely me running from myself.

Karl's addictions had become cars and watches. He now looks back and sees that he was trying to fill the void with materialistic things. My addiction was moving houses, and his was purchases. Neither made us feel any better in the long term, and all we did was waste time, money, and cause extra stress to our lives.

How many of us have an addiction to something in our lives, and when we look deep within, can to see that the addiction is merely a way of us stopping and connecting deeply with ourselves? Social media has caused so many more of us to stop doing the very things that bring us joy, and they are disconnecting us from each other as well as ourselves. Only recently Karl and I decided to remove TV and electronics in the week (other than for work). After five years, Karl has finally picked up the guitar that he promised himself he would learn to play. The children are picking up their instruments more, we are playing more games together, and although Seren at first said I had ruined her life, I am loving how she sits on my bed each night and talks to me about her day, her friends, and how she is feeling. In contrast, before she locked herself away with her iPhone. The change so far has been wonderful.

The average person will touch their phone almost 2,700 times a day. A full 10% of people will touch their phones over 5,400 times a day. As I write this book, I have taken myself off social media and now only use my phone to check the weather, listen to music, use my meditation app, or check emails. It has freed up so much time, and I highly suggest you do the same to free up some of your creativity and healing, Try journalling instead of scrolling. Use your *Heal The Mother Journal* to see the magic and the lessons unfold. Find yourself again. What do you love? What have you stopped doing that brought you so much joy? Start to write about this in your journal and then make the changes that your heart desires. It won't be easy, and at first, your children will struggle, but eventually, it will become the new normal, and you will thank your lucky stars that you made these changes.

Not all people who are awakening are lost or are suffering; this was just my journey and is the journey for so many of us. However, there are other different ways that an awakening can happen. In this chapter, I will share three with you—mine, my husband's, and my cousin Vikki's. I have just spent the afternoon with Vikki after not seeing her for ten years. We finally caught up in Sydney on this road trip, as my inner guide and intuition told me very clearly that I needed to contact her and see her. My aim in this book is to help you awaken and begin to be led by your heart. I want you to be guided by love, to discover how to connect with your intuition, and to be guided by your higher self—the part of you that is plugged into the universe. The reason I am so passionate about helping you with this is that I didn't have this support. I was hurtling down a roller-coaster without a seatbelt, trying all sorts of healing modalities, learning different types of spirituality methods. Along the way, I picked up lots of myths and fears from others.

Finding My Tribe

I searched for a long time to find my people. I had a deep knowing and desire to be with other women in a circle under the moonlight. I had a desire to be in this space, to share, to open our hearts, to heal, and to weep together. I had no idea where I would find a group like that, but my soul yearned for it. I had just come back from travelling around Byron Bay in a campervan, and it was there that I was first introduced to crystals and the hippie way of living. Seren has been obsessed with crystals since she was a toddler. She had a big range of crystals and would always seek out amethysts. Many children and young people are also connected with crystals, nature, and animals in a way very different from how we were raised. They have a deeper knowing, and when we trust, we can learn so much from them. It was, in fact, Seren who helped me connect with this part of myself. My soul yearned to be connected and to find a tribe of women who would help me on this journey of spirituality.

Years before I was a Hypnobirthing practitioner, and before we left for Australia, I connected with a Hypnobirthing practitioner in Perth called Diana. I told her I was moving to Perth and was hoping to start Hypnobirthing teaching again as I had just had two incredible births close together. I told her that once we became settled in Australia, I would like to begin teaching parent classes again. Funny enough, I ended up by complete chance bumping into Diana years later at the children's school. It was the most unbelievable moment as Diana's children didn't even go to that school, and she had come by chance to visit her best friend after school. These

> Always trust that the intentions you set and the dreams you have for yourself can be delivered to you through the universe when you trust and believe with your heart.

two women—Diana and Nat—have become two of my dearest friends. By complete chance, they too yearned for a women's circle, so months after we met, they created our own full moon women's circle, which is still going strong three years later.

Birthing Our Sister Circle

During the time that we started the women's circle, I also began going to church. I had a two-year love affair with a local Pentecostal church I stumbled across completely by accident. I hadn't really connected with God until that point, always the universe, but I had never explored the connection that we have to God. I had always prayed and got married in church and had my babies christened, but I wasn't sure why. Maybe I felt that is just what we did? Some of my family are devout Catholics and have always had a strong connection with the church. Their religion had always been a huge part of their life, but for me, in many ways, I found that it was too confining for me to feel it fully in my heart.

However, this church felt very different. It wasn't about religion *per se*; it felt more about spirituality and finding our divine purpose. The pastors shared Scripture from the Bible, but they also weaved in modern-day suffering of addiction and mental health issues. They would offer powerful prayer circles and healings at the end of the service, and there was something about it, that brought me comfort and a sense of belonging,

They had a beautiful kids' church, where the children would go and play for two hours every Sunday, and I would listen to the powerful sermons. I would sing, dance, pray, and cry, and through this new weekly practise, I started to soften and feel lighter. I would feel an energy every time I walked in, which I have never felt before in a church.

I started to allow myself to connect with that part of me that lay dormant for so long. I felt like I began to connect with my soul and a power far greater than me. I would have full-body goosebumps whilst I was singing, and at times during the Sermon, it would feel as though the Pastors words were just for me. His words made such sense, and I would feel a little bit more connected, healed, and happier each time I would go.

Connecting with The Divine

During this time, I began to hear thoughts that didn't feel like mine. They felt beautiful, soft, and full of love. I guess my understanding is that I started to hear the words of God. For me, it was like a knowing, and it felt different from my busy thoughts. Many people believe it's God, other people feel it's spirit, angels, guides, or their higher selves, but for me, I feel like it all comes from the same one true source—which is love.

One Sunday, whilst listening to the sermon, I felt my heart chakra burst open as the pastor asked God to speak to me, I heard words as clear as day. 'Help them, Susy. Help the women and children'. It was so profound that I cried uncontrollably throughout the next two hours. I continuously sobbed each time I went to church. It was like all the hurt and pain within was flooding out, and through the tears, the sorrow left my aching heart. It was at this point in my life that I decided to openly and proudly share our story with ADHD and how we had overcome the hard times and helped our beautiful daughter learn to thrive in life.

At the same time, I was also learning to meditate. I came across a meditation teacher online who again blew my heart chakra wide open. I would sit through the meditations and weep. There was so much pain that needed to come out. I needed to heal my aching heart so I could once again connect with my inner guidance and light the way of the path that had become darkened over time.

I went to women's circles, I saged, and I used my crystals and had healing upon healing. What I didn't realise is that I was entering what is known as a healing crisis or spiritual emergency. I was hurtling even further into the spiritual abyss, walking around with my chakras wide open. I didn't understand how to protect my energy or how to clear my energy. I was walking around like a spiritual vacuum sucking in energy from everywhere and anywhere. Once your chakras start to activate and open, we must be wise and learn how to protect ourselves. Sometimes, when we activate the light within us, we shine so brightly that other energies may be attracted to us. Like a moth drawn to a lightbulb, we can become a beacon for all. The Bible and Christians will refer to it as the devil; I like to think of it as people who have come to your dinner party without being asked. I am going to give you the tools to ask them to leave lovingly, and through this vibration, they will move with love and grace. I truly believe that so many people are walking around with energy that simply isn't theirs, even children. There is a way to free themselves of this energy. They can ask that their energy and their light is returned to them—it really is that simple. I have created a meditation to help you with this stage which you can find in Chapter 10. It's called 'Cutting Chords with Archangel Michael'.

The Healing Crisis

As I unknowingly started to enter my healing crisis, I became very anxious. I remember being very tearful, and I had also been diagnosed with ADHD and PMDD (more about this in Chapter 3), so throwing this into the mix was now hurtling me full throttle and deep into fear. The more fear I felt, the more fear I attracted and the more healing I sort out.

After being diagnosed with ADHD, my daughter Seren was still going to all her appointments and was on her healing journey. We had just embarked on a series of neurofeedback sessions which can support children with ADHD without medication. I decided to have a QEEG scan which identified some interesting things that I will share with you in Chapter 6. It was after my neurofeedback session that things started to get weird. For Seren (and almost everyone else on the planet), neurofeedback has only a positive outcome. But, for me and with all my ongoing healings and spiritual work, it took me down a strange rabbit hole!

We noticed a positive difference in Seren that evening, and while I was super tired, I felt fine. I fell asleep early and then woke at midnight with crippling anxiety. I was tossing and turning and had no idea why I felt that way. I am super sensitive even with coffee, but this felt like I'd had twelve cans of Red Bull. My thoughts were racing, my heart was pounding, and I had an overwhelming feeling of not being safe, even though I was my own home. I am going to share all this with you as there are so many people who may have experienced something similar. I want you to know that you aren't going mad! It's quite the opposite; like with Neo in *The Matrix*, you are simply waking up. That doesn't mean it will happen to everyone, which is the reason I will be sharing two other awakenings with you.

That night was very eerie for me. I remember lying on the sofa with my gorgeous dog, Chip, and looking out the huge glass doors in the lounge at the night sky. It was a full moon, and as the moonlight illuminated the clouds, they were changing shape and becoming like scary monster faces. Was this what it was like to be a five-year-old? What was happening to me? It was like I'd taken some weird psychedelic drugs.

Listening to episode after episode of Oprah's *Soul Conversation* podcast and hearing Tony Robbins' words about the power of the heart and how it is even more powerful than the mind is something that has always stayed with me. Never forget that everything happens to us for a reason. There is a greater plan for all of us, and these seemingly challenging moments happen for a reason. Choosing to ignore the anxiety, heavy chest, and eerie clouds, and listening to Tony Robbins' words helped me to feel safe. Hugging my dog close to me, I began to fall asleep just as the sun started to rise.

The next day and night were just as bad. I felt scared, like I didn't know myself, and when I started to pray, I felt darkness over me, blocking me from connecting with Source. The beautiful and loving energy I had been connecting with suddenly felt blocked, and it scared me. It was the dark night of the soul, but I believe it was my time to awaken, even though it felt completely out of my control. What I have learned on this journey is that spirituality is a beautiful thing, but sometimes it will take you on paths you never knew existed. Those calm rivers can turn into dangerous waterfalls and rapids no one told you about, so I am here to guide you lovingly through those times and to give you some extra paddles, extra lifejackets, and some training in rapid waterfalls. I want to provide you with a roadmap, a plan, and a loving guide to help you navigate these beautiful, yet powerful AF waters.

I want to honour you for being brave enough to do this work. So many wouldn't even so much as dip their toe in these waters, so always know you are incredible for giving yourself this gift of life as it is meant to be travelled. We were always meant for an awakened life which is why so many children are born 'awake', but sadly their truth and sovereignty can be simply brainwashed out of them. You should remember that however crazy it gets, on the other side is a blissful awakened life where you genuinely learn not only to heal but to discover your true path in this life.

Over the next few days and weeks, I realised I was becoming increasingly anxious and not wanting to spend any time with friends or school mums. I felt so out of my rhythm that I needed to stay indoors. I also learned I had high levels of histamine in my body through the QEEG scan, and I needed to go on a low histamine diet. That consisted of taking out all my favourite foods and eliminating caffeine and alcohol. At the time, it felt horrific, but what it did is give me the gift of learning to sit with and be myself without using the crutch of alcohol or coffee. Getting rid of both of those crutches for a while and changing my diet allowed me to say goodbye at last to some crippling anxiety I had been feeling for a long time. I had gone for the QEEG to support Seren as we were discovering ways to help her manage her ADHD. Through supporting Seren, and entirely by accident I realised why I'd had such crippling anxiety for so long.

I used to wake up and feel the anxiety as soon as I opened my eyes. I would then make a flat white coffee which would add to my anxiety. In the evening, a glass or two of wine would take the edge off, but it would be back full force the next morning, and so it would continue. There are so many of us living like that, which is why so many of us are taking medication. I fell into that trap too. There are many different reasons we are feeling this anxiety and many various tools that will support you to get rid of it, but you will find none of them at the doctor's office. I feel modern-day medicine simply blocks us from feeling and allowing the release of stagnant and suppressed emotions. Sure, there is a place for it, but I think we all know as a collective we are relying on pharmaceutical drugs way too much.

I will be sharing with you some tools to help with your anxiety and those that have helped me almost eliminate it from my life. Part of my awakening was allowing myself to see what the anxiety was trying to teach me. I began to pull away from friends who didn't make me feel good about myself. I started to distance myself from low energy conversations about fear, ridicule of others, and unkind behaviour.

Don't waste your beautiful energy on people who don't make you feel like the sunlight.

The Start of My Metamorphosis

I have always loved being the centre of attention, and now I couldn't even go along to a school mums' dinner. I began worrying that I had some sort of social anxiety but then decided only to allow myself to research spiritual meanings and not diagnoses. I needed to be connecting with people and messages online of only the highest good to bring me back to love; I needed to trust.

I began to avoid situations that didn't make me feel good. I began to distance myself from situations where I always said yes instead of no. It was one of the hardest things I have ever done. I have always been a people pleaser, but now I understand this can happen to those of us who have had difficult or strict childhoods. We could never please our parents, so in adulthood, we try and please others, but the more we do that, the more we are not honouring our higher selves. We are merely living someone else's life and being how others want us to act, which is never good because, in the end, we lose our sense of self.

I also discovered that my anxiety showed its head again when I was totally out of alignment with who I was. Who I had become was not what I truly needed or wanted. I genuinely believe anxiety can be our internal guide to wake us up to the suffering and pain that needs healing. It's our internal gauge trying to tell us that something is not right.

If this is you right now, please start to use the healing tools for mama at the back of the book along with daily future-self journalling. I share in Chapter 10 in detail how future self-journalling is a powerful yet simple tool for creating change, especially around mental health. I also want you to honour yourself and your journey and trust and know that we are going through a mass awakening all over the planet right now. We are awakening faster and at a more unprecedented pace than we have ever known before, and I want you to trust in the process. Trust all the lessons, trust your intuition, and listen to those whispers of the soul that are trying to reach you and bring you home. As you go on this journey, you will start to heal in a way you never imagined possible and remember you are not alone. A Course in Miracles tells us that anxiety and feeling overwhelmed can be a true sign that you are relying on your strength. Know that your higher self is always trying to call you forward and align you back to love. You have angels and guides always working on your behalf, helping you and healing you. We all have different beliefs, and you should always do what feels congruent to you in your heart. I use prayer for different things. As we are told from *A Course in Miracles*, prayer is the medium for miracles. I have learned that when we put our pain and suffering up to God, the universe, or our guides and angels, miracles can happen. I have experienced it so much in the past five years, and I have witnessed, seen, and felt the power of the supernatural. I will be giving you tools in Chapter 7 that will help you begin to connect with your guides, your angels, your higher self, and let go of anything that doesn't serve you. I will lovingly guide and support you to bring you home to your truth, so you begin to allow the magic to unfold in your life.

We Are All Connected

I want to share with you two other awakenings that I have witnessed. Unlike mine, they didn't come in the form of their child's behaviour or through mental health struggles. Theirs were completely different, and it's worth sharing as so many awakenings come wearing different masks. You must understand what can happen when you remove your mask.

Karl's awakening came in the form of an eight-week man's course that I bought him for Christmas. Karl is a confident, successful, and fantastic guy who achieves everything he sets out to do. Karl has never had any type of mental health issues and not once has he ever felt even the slightest bit of anxiety. He is amazing, and in my twenty years of loving him, every time anyone asks how he is, he always says, 'I'm fantastic'! However, he had very little compassion for anyone struggling with mental health and saw it as a sign of weakness. We always used to joke, and I would tell Karl that he was as 'shallow as nat's piss'. I loved him dearly, but there was no depth at all to his emotional pool.

We had been on different spiritual paths for the last few years. I was awakening, learning about God, spirit guides and praying, and Karl had slowly become more of an atheist after watching a series of documentaries on YouTube. One night I could see and feel how much he needed more of a spiritual connection, even if he didn't.

For the last five years since selling his business, Karl had told me that he was always asking, 'Is this it'? Even though he would go on many different adventures with us and by himself or with friends, it seemed he was still searching. He felt that when he sold his business, he would stop working and start surfing, but what he came to realise is that not having a purpose in life was disconnecting him further from himself. I could feel it and see it, but he couldn't. I thought that he was searching for something that he was never going to find because he wasn't going inwards, but instead outwards with adventures and material purchases.

I loved Karl with all my heart and truly wanted him to be happy, so I suggested that if after the course, he still didn't feel right, he could travel for three months alone. I don't know why I said it, and I am not sure I truly meant it. I guess I was simply trying to figure out what he needed. I always felt that maybe the children and I weren't enough for him, but even he didn't know the answer.

The men's course ripped Karl's heart out, cracked him wide open and knocked the wind of out his sails. I have never seen him cry like that before. He cried every single day for two weeks. It was a deeply confronting and soul-expanding eight weeks of releasing guilt, shame, fear, unprocessed pain, and everything else in between. It changed him more than I could have ever imagined; it brought him home to himself. Once again, we were able to have conversations about the universe, spirituality, and although we have very different beliefs of what God meant, to be able to connect with him on this deeper level was beautiful. We would talk about our childhoods, and for the first time, he had compassion for mine and could understand why I had struggled over the years. He softened. He glowed, and almost immediately, things started to change for both of us in a way neither of us expected.

Karl's entire life since the age of eleven was repressing his feelings of pain over his father leaving. They were buried deep within, hidden by a mask of happiness. What Karl came to realise is that we when we suppress emotions of pain, we suppress everything else too, including feelings of pure joy and tender moments with loved ones. None of them could ever be deeply felt. He started to realise that when he faced his pain and released it, inside was so much emotion that he finally allowed himself to feel. Like so many of us, pain and sadness can be experienced in childhood, and that is why this work is so important. Whether this suffering came from a parental break up, bullying, self-esteem issues, problems at school, death of a loved one or some type of abuse, for many of us, we have simply buried it away and allowed ourselves not to feel it.

The gift that we have of time on this earth is that we can heal together. There are so many of us going through a collective spiritual awakening, yet many do not speak of it. However, when we start to lean in and do the work, you and the others will find each other. The light will pull us together wherever we are in the world. As I close this chapter, I want to share with you my final story of an awakening. Remember, no two stories are the same, but I want you to know and understand that while the medical world has lots of diagnoses, that model does not support the reality of a spiritual awakening.

Remember what I said about the greatest gurus of all time? I told you that if their spiritual awakenings occurred in the Western World, they would have been locked up in a mental institution, but, as they happened in the Eastern world, they were simply left alone. Try and remember this as you are going through your journey. Once you understand and start to believe you aren't going mad, you can allow yourself to surrender and soften with the journey. Moving back the last of the autumn leaves and debris after the long, harsh winter will allow your light to be seen finally, like the first rays of the sun after a long winter.

You begin to trust, let go of logic, and walk bravely into the path of the unknown—for it is here that you will find yourself buried amongst the earth.

The Power of The Heart

I want to share with you my cousin Vikki's awakening. We lived on either side of Australia and even though I had visited over east a few times, we hadn't seen each other in over ten years. We have had several road trips over the last few years, and this time Australia was going through some of the worst bush fires ever recorded. Sydney plummeted into near-total darkness. A thick hazy fog engulfed Sydney, and the air quality was toxic. We had planned to go to Sydney, but due to the raging bush fires, we decided that we wouldn't visit the national parks there this time. I messaged Vikki and told her that sadly we wouldn't be visiting.

Out of the blue just a couple of months before, Vikki had called me to say to me she was going through an awakening. We hadn't spoken other than messages on social media, but she had been reading my blogs and felt connected to my message of *Heal The Mother, Heal The Child.* Even though I had a messaged her saying we wouldn't be going, I had a constant voice telling me that I needed to go. Later in this book, I will share some incredible and daunting things that have been happening to me this year, so when I had this constant voice, I knew it was one of my guides telling me I needed to go. I will draw on this in more detail later, but that deep knowing, that direct thought, and feeling of certainty told me I had to go.

A couple of days before that, I had booked a campsite near to the Sydney northern beaches and then messaged Vikki saying we were coming to see her. She was delighted and sent me her address inviting us over for a swim and pizza. I couldn't believe that the campsite I booked was only a few kilometres away from Vikki's house! Of all the places in the world, we had chosen a campsite just around the corner from her. That was also a sign for me that I was right to listen to my inner guidance. When it comes from a place of love, and when I feel it deeply, I trust it. Some call it intuition, others their higher self, but for me, I see it as my guides, and I trust those nudges! They always get it right, and when I don't listen, I still know they were right.

It's important to remember that when I began this journey, my thoughts were ego-based and fear-driven. They were almost as frantic as my actions, so don't worry if you aren't feeling the connection with my story right now. This book will give you the steps to get to that point.

It was amazing to see Vikki. We both had a deep connection with our late Grandma Peggy, and when I saw Vikki, I instantly felt close to Grandma. I am sure she felt the same way about me. We went through similarly challenging childhoods, but the one thing that was consistent for both of us was our love and support from our grandparents. As we sat and chatted over pizza, Vikki started to share with Karl and me what had recently happened to her. She had been to an incredible weekend event which worked to unblock the chakras in the body. The workshop explained that healing can come through the body when we change the way our minds perceive things. It also revealed that pain, suffering and trauma could cause such illness in the body. The speaker shared how his mother had been able to heal her cancer by allowing the pain of losing her son to be healed. He shared how his mother had lost her baby son when she was younger. She still held the pain in her heart, and he realised that to heal her body, she needed to heal her heart. Once she was able to do this, along with other such things, she was able to take steps to begin healing her cancer.

During this weekend, Vikki told me she realised that her throat chakra was so blocked and that was why she felt that for so long she couldn't find her voice. I, too, have struggled with that in the past. Part of this work has meant I was finally able to find my true voice. Vikki told me that she felt all over that her chakras became wide open, and from that point, everything started to change.

Vikki told us she was walking through the forest near her house one day when she had a moment of deep knowing, that aha moment and realization that we all get to when allowing the light to shine out of hearts. When we allow ourselves to be freed from the shackles of conditioning, lies and untruths that were indoctrinated into us, we can finally see the light.

She started to understand that everything comes from the heart, and it is from there that we must connect, not with our heads. At that moment, she was able to witness the incredible magnitude and beauty of the woods. It was so striking to her that she sat down on a rock and started to sob uncontrollably. She asked the universe for a sign to show her that humanity had a heart, and then a couple ran over to her to see if she was ok. She said that confirmed her belief in society, and if we can heal the heart, we can heal the world. Just thinking about this right now makes me see this too. We are living in a male-dominated world, and we know this part of both men and women can bring control and fear as it leads with the head. To bring the feminine essence, strength, and power back to our communities that they so need, we must start feeling and leading with our hearts.

Vikki had a realisation that we are creating so much suffering in this world because humanity hasn't yet found the one thing that it's already within us. The depth of suffering is because we are so disconnected from ourselves. She realised that we are killing ourselves and the planet because we have moved so far away from who we truly are and who we are truly meant to be, yet, we are slowly awakening to the power and beauty and love within us. The magnitude of this hit Vikki so much, and the deep sobs coming from her body were for humanity. She felt like she was letting go of the hurt, fear, and sadness she'd absorbed from what she'd just discovered. It was this discovery that really catapulted Vikki into discovering her true purpose.

I know Vikki is only at the start of her journey, and everything is changing around her now from her relationship with her family to her relationship with her children. She sees and feels the massive impact that pain and suffering can have not only on our hearts, but also on our children, and that is why it's so important for us to do the work.

Each time we heal ourselves, we send a vibration out to mothers across the globe. We are one, we are all connected, and when we collectively heal our hearts, we began to heal the heart and soul of Mother Earth.

Spiritual Upgrades

Over the last few years since my initial awakening, I have had what I feel are upgrades. Each time, I have started to feel anxious, lonely, or disconnected, I now understand that this is part of the process. I welcome the lessons, I allow myself to go inwards, and I trust that I am healing, shedding, and ascending. Remember, life isn't only about the wins and those love and light moments. It is also about going through the darkness and pain to get to the light. We can try and outrun the darkness, but eventually, it will catch up. That for me is where the problem with society lies. We are not given tools to cope with these times other than a redirection of the thoughts and pain, or self-medicating to cope. We also have a medical system that doesn't support healing, but instead brushes issues under the carpet with medication and encourages 'conceal, don't feel'. I trust everything now, every single thing, and I see all of it as a lesson.

I had a family falling out recently, and it although it came from nowhere, I know what triggered it. I can now see all the lessons and understand that the person may have deep, unhealed wounds. They are not prepared to see this, so instead, I have suffered some very heavy and unkind emails. Years ago, that would have thrown me. I would have reacted and allowed it to consume my thoughts and conversation. In this space of healing, I can witness that this is their pain, not mine, and my daughter has just been the trigger to bring this to the surface. I have been able to respond with love and kindness and not allow the negativity to lower my vibration.

Yes, it has been painful, and yes, it has been complicated over Christmas and New Year, but I am trusting with all my heart that there is something bigger at place happening. A force greater than all of us is always working on our behalf and trying to bring us back to love. I have been incredibly proud of myself in how I have been able to handle the situation with grace and love.

Once we begin to heal, once we can see the triggers and honour our boundaries instead of creating fear-based boundaries, we can handle all conflict and darkness with trust, love, and faith—that is my wish for you, my friend.

CHAPTER 3
HEALING THE WOMB TO UNLOCK YOUR FEMININE POWER.

I struggled with my periods since the age of fifteen. I remember my mother taking me to the doctor and saying, 'Please, help her doctor'. Little did we know back then that the womb holds not only our pain but ancestral trauma. Once we set the curse free, she becomes our powerful, secret chalice to the soul, to our creativity, and to our sacred feminine wisdom.

For 25 years, I suffered from my periods; it didn't feel like a period, but more like a curse. I would loathe them, fear them, even dread them, but little did I know that some of our deepest pain is held in our womb. It is also the place where we hold our most incredible power and our ancestral imprinting. We can hold onto pain and emotional trauma passed down from generations without even realising it, but this sacred womb space can also hold some of our ancestral gifts. It is from the bowl of creation and love that we can harness our greatest power. It is from this place that we can truly remember who we are and learn to embody the sacred and potent power. Firstly, we must shed and let go of pain, suffering, guilt, shame and fear to be able to grow in love and depth from this sacred vault.

In the last twelve months, I learned that not only all my pain, suffering, and trauma, but also that of my mother, grandmothers, and right up the ancestral line was buried deep within my womb. I pray this hasn't entered my daughters' wombs, as I only learned about this work after I had given birth to them. I trust that if they do struggle, I will be able to help them to heal. I fully embody the notion that we are more than our bodies. We have an energetic and karmic field that goes far beyond ourselves. This magical thread can be woven into the very fabric and makeup of our children. I am trusting that by working on myself and my ancestral line, it will also clear their energy and allow their wombs to fill only with light, not suffering.

If I have learned anything, it's that we can change our environment through our thought patterns. We are able through the law of attraction to create love, abundance, and joy, not only in our hearts and minds but in those of our children. I discovered through my parenting that what we hold in our hearts for our child, our child will create for us. If we want to change our child, we must change the thoughts, words and actions that we have about them. Not always easy, believe me I know this better than anyone, but when I had a bleak view of Seren's future which was brought on by negativity from society, teachers and peers, that is exactly what the universe brought me—in abundance. Karl and I had to radically change the way we thought about our daughter's future, and in doing this, everything began to change. I would meditate every day and only allow myself to see positive images and stories around Seren; this practise became so powerful that her behaviour began to change in the most magical of ways. Karl and I try so hard to watch what we say about our children because the universe

> We must not allow the critical voice to dampen the spirits of our children. We must talk kindly, compassionately, and lovingly about them as the universe is always listening (and so are they).

brings us what we ask for, so let's make it abundant and magical and not fear-based and negative.

Fearing My Monthly Cycle

Almost three years ago, I discovered that my monthly menstruation suffering was in fact, given a label of PMDD, which is how the medical world describes it. There is a long list of characteristics about the condition, and still very little is known about it. It can be a serious condition and something that shouldn't be taken lightly. But I had a deep knowing that it was in my life for a reason, and there was more to it than I was being told.

I have a strong belief that for many women, PMDD can come from unhealed abuse, trauma, and pain, which doesn't always have to be ours; it can be passed down through epigenetics. Dr. Gabor Mate tells us he experienced that, and through his mother's trauma and depression, it was weaved into him. He suffered addiction issues and was also diagnosed with ADHD but was able to heal himself when he understood that his pain and addiction issues were trauma. In his four decades of work as a physician, he said that every addict he had worked with has suffered trauma and the addiction is a symptom of unhealed pain and suffering. If you want to understand this concept further, there is a fantastic documentary called *In Utero*. I was so fascinated by this movie that I screened it at a local cinema. I wanted to share this with as many women as possible, and the cinema was full, with a large waiting list. This shows me how much we are waking up and wanting to understand the work of epigenetics more and more. We understand we cannot keep passing trauma down the ancestral line. It is time to feel it and heal it.

I suffered from PMDD for more than 25 years. Twenty-five years of monthly suffering, crying, shaming myself, and hurting myself both emotionally and physically. Twenty-five years of feeling like a complete psychopath and loathing my periods and myself. I only learned it was PMDD when I was 40 years old;

it was the same time that I was diagnosed with ADHD. I was told at the time that there wasn't a lot known about PMDD, and the best thing for me would be to take medication. I did my research and learned that you could take medication for two weeks out of the month, so two weeks on and two weeks off, but I learned from many women that even this didn't seem to work.

Is Medication the Answer?

You see, that's the thing about medication. Sure, it has a place in society as do blue socks, but it doesn't mean it can fix our life's problems. It can also bring side effects, and then you need medication for the side effects and so on and so forth. Having gone through a period of taking medication, I came to learn that as soon as I stopped the drug, the problem was still there. I truly believe our body knows when we are out of alignment, which is why we feel anxious, depressed, hormonal, and have brain fog, etc. It is our body trying to tell us we have a dis-ease with the body and mind. It's sending alarms bell, and when we listen to our intuition and trust her, we can begin our healing process. For so long, society has wanted to fix it straight away. We aren't taught to sit in the uncomfortableness of our feelings. We are taught that we must see someone, fix it, make it go away, or appear normal, but that tells our intuition it's not good enough, that we should be quiet and not allow our inner feelings to be seen, heard, or validated. The more we push those feelings aside, and the more we repress them, the bigger the pain-body grows.

What I have also learned over the last few years is that our pain body can be transferred onto our children. Through epigenetics, those anxieties, fears, shame and guilt can be passed on to our unborn babies. That also applies to previous generations. If you allow yourself to think what the female ancestral line has witnessed in their lives, you can understand how we can be feeling as we do this now. Famine, war, repression, male dominance, and abuse in many different forms; it's horrific when you think what the women in our ancestral line have been through. If we go further back, we can understand about witch-hunting, and women being burned at stake, it's shocking to think that happened to women. The sad thing is that it is still happening in many different countries across the globe. Right now, the world is going through such a huge, painful awakening. It's been a hard time to learn about the atrocities that are playing out in the world towards women and children, but the more the light is shined on the darkness, the more we can make a change as a collective. Women across the globe are fighting back, fighting for their rights, pulling together, refusing to be silenced, and rising!

My dream is that this book helps you to heal, regain your power, and rise! There is much work needed to be done on this planet, and as the Dalai Lama said at a peace conference in 2014, the western woman will save the world. When I read his words, I feel into it. Yes, we have our issues, but we are safer than most of the women across the world. We don't have extreme poverty, famine and war like so many other countries do. We have women's rights, and even when at times they are stripped away from us, we come together and fight for them as we are seeing happen across the world. We are seeing women fight for justice for their children, raising awareness about vaccinations, child trafficking and fighting hard to change laws. Women are a powerful force to be reckoned with (but first, we must deal with the ancestral trauma and self-limiting beliefs that are holding us back). I am also seeing a rise in men supporting women and standing tall raising awareness alongside us. Men see our pleas, our fights, our values for freedom and choice, and they are rising with us, and this is a beautiful thing to see.

Healing Our Birth Trauma

Our mother's birth trauma or the birth trauma of our children can be held within the womb. Sexual, emotional, and physical trauma can also be energetically held in that sacred space. My intention with this chapter is to get you reacquainted with your womb space. I want to help you begin to let go of any of the trauma and teach you how to turn this scared chalice into your deepest love and hub of creativity, magic, and wonder! For years, I struggled with PMDD, but I didn't understand it; I didn't realise what it was. I hated my periods, for they would change me from a happy-go-lucky person, into an anxious, angry, and violent shadow of myself. I see now that was I harbouring so much in that space. When I would have my period, instead of letting her teach me what we needed to release, I went further into anger and sadness.

I went further and further into despair, and each month, I would start panicking as I began to ovulate. I would feel the distant emotions of anger, anxiety, and self-loathing, and would worry that powerful wrath of her power was only two short weeks away. I would create stories in my head that weren't true. I would start to feel the shadows of myself, and my ego would become louder and louder.

You are a failure. Who will listen to you? Why are you doing this work? You are a bad mother. You are not loveable. I hate you. As the days from ovulation to menstruation would grow closer, the ego and the shadows would get louder. They would get so loud that I would start listening, they would win, and I would find myself crying for days on end. I would take myself off social media, I wouldn't plan anything, I would cancel appointments, and I would start to dislike Karl. I would feel that we were drifting, or that he didn't love me, and I would question why we were together. He would remind me I have been the same for the last twenty years, and he would tell me I was needy, and that would make me retreat further into my shell of self-loathing. I would try and get through the school run as best I could and hurry the kids into the car, fearing I would make eye contact with one of the other school mums. That is coming from a mum who would happily stay at school after pick up until dinner time chatting and laughing with all the mums and children. So, to have such a change in personality was challenging, as friends would notice the profound change in me.

I am the mum who usually loves sitting on the grass while the kids play. I chat with other school mums about kids, spiritual awakenings, and channelling (I am so thankful for some of the mums at our school). So, you can imagine how strange it was to me that I would become the mum that couldn't even bear thinking of talking to anyone during that time. I would be continuously triggered by everyone—the people in the shops, social media, my kids, my husband, and my family. Each time I was triggered, instead of seeing the triggers as the guides, I would see them as people being unkind to me. My ego would tell me even more, that I was not enough, and that no one liked me. It was relentless, and I would start to believe the once silent whispers that now became screams.

Often, we need to go through the hardships, confusion, and darkness to get to the light and discover our dreams.

Listening to My Inner Mean Girl

Each month, like a cycle of doom, I would hear the words over and over in my head. *You are a failure.* I would get through as best as I could during this time—eat, sleep, snuggle with the kids in pyjamas after school pick up, and often order take-aways as I couldn't even imagine beginning to think about dinner. It was like hormonal bipolar, and one of the reasons I am sharing this is that one out of twenty women have PMDD, and many of these women don't realise they have it. It's essential to raise awareness but also to give you the tools that have helped me so you can use them for yourself, your daughters, and other women you know who are struggling. It's about supporting each other, loving each other, holding space for one another without judgment, and guiding each other to come back to love over fear.

As soon as I got my diagnosis, I was told by the psychologist that the psychiatrist would be in touch. Like many experts here in Perth, he had a twelve-month waiting list, but I was told that because I was being referred, I should be able to get an appointment very soon. To be honest, I knew deep within my heart that this path wouldn't be for me. I had just spent nine months trying to readjust after being on an antidepressant for five months, so the last thing I wanted was more medication. It helped me greatly at the time when I felt I needed something quick and effective, but that was a time when I was in the cultural mindset that I need an instant and quick fix. I had no other tools to help, guide and support me, so medication was the only thing that I knew of that may be able to help. I feel there is a place for medicine, but I also didn't understand that to heal, I would need to sit through the pain and discomfort of my feelings. Don't get me wrong, there are times in life when we need the support of medication, and there should be no judgment. But sadly, so many adults and children are being prescribed medication they often don't need. My doctor at the time urged me not to take medication (which is very rare today). He advised me that I was struggling to parent my child and 9000 miles away from home in a new country with a young family. He was right, but at the time I simply needed a buoyancy aid to keep me afloat through the thick and hazy fog while I tried to navigate the journey.

Shortly after my diagnosis of ADHD and PMDD, things started to get worse before they got better. My brain fog became so bad I found it so difficult to concentrate. It would make me so annoyed with myself as I couldn't remember what I was doing. I would forget appointments, school meetings, play dates and then hate myself even more. I would feel so overwhelmed that I couldn't make decisions. I would chop and change what I wanted to do with my business, but also, I hadn't made peace with myself. I always wished I could be someone else. My self-esteem was shot. I started to read everything and anything that I could on self-healing. I read Louise Hay's *You Can Heal Your Life* and *Dying to Be Me* by Anita Moorjani. I began to start to put in some self-care, and for the first time, I began to meditate daily. My meditations would always be guided. I would choose ones that would talk about manifesting, creating the life we want, and so on and so forth, but I have since learned that is like trying to build a home without first laying down the foundations. As soon as we have a fierce storm, our house is going to blow over and be destroyed, and that is what was happening to me. I was trying to skip past go without playing by the rules. You must do the hard work first—lay the foundations, heal your inner child, work on your shadows, heal the mother and father wounds, and allow the brokenness to be fixed. When we do this, our light can once again shine out to the world.

Healing Your Bowl of Light

There is an old Hawaiian story that says when we are born, we have a bowl of light in our base chakra. This bowl of light is our divine connection to source, and this thread connects us to our higher self. Our higher self is based on love, and it is our true connection to the divine. As children begin their lives, many parents, caregivers and teachers unintentionally start to condition them out of this connection with the divine. They begin to learn that they are not good enough, that the world is a scary and hostile place, and questions such as why is the sky blue and why do elephants have trunks, change drastically. Children are shamed, bullied, coerced, and each time they face negativity from the outside world, their bowl of light starts to fill up with pebbles. As they come into adulthood, they can face further judgment and comparison, and then more and more pebbles enter their bowl of light. The bowl of light can now be full of pebbles, and their connection with their higher self and reason for their incarnation on this earth dims more and more. We have not been taught how to remove those pebbles, and then we find ourselves broken, lost, anxious, and living a life so far removed from ourselves that our light is now dim. My intention with this book is to give you the tools so you can start to remove those pebbles and your bowl of light can once again shine out to the world, and you remember who you are in this life.

I started to meditate daily, but I knew I needed more. After I read *Dying To Be Me*, I realised I had spent my entire adult life being unkind to myself. I spoke unkind words to myself that would permeate deeply into my cells. If I think back to my childhood and the lack of emotional stability, emotional neglect, and fear-based learning, no wonder I lacked in love and respect for myself. I am not blaming my mother for her actions—that was all she knew, and she was doing the best she could at the time. She had her own issues from her childhood, and she was born in a time of survival during the end of the war. There wasn't time to work on our own emotional needs; we just had to get on with it. I don't blame my dad either, and I see that even though I didn't have a stable base at home, I had terrific grandparents who gave me so much time, love, and support. I have so much gratitude in my heart for them; they saved me in so many ways.

The Olden Days

My dad always said that my grandmother was stoic; she just got on with life. She would tell me stories of post-war hard-ships. She told me how she lost the true love of her life in the war, and when my granddad asked for her hand in marriage, she told him she didn't love him because she loved the man lost in the war. My grandad assured her he had enough love for both, so she agreed. She also yearned for a daughter but was only blessed with two sons. She would always tell me how she was so sad she didn't have a daughter and would tell me I was like the daughter she never had. I always wondered if deep down, this would have affected her boys in some way? We now understand the impact of our emotions and thoughts and how they can impact our children. I know I do this with my spirited child. I may act a certain way towards her, but my thoughts are different at times, and I know her energy will be able to pick it up. I feel that one of the gifts of healing is that even if I have made mistakes with Seren, I am open to doing all the healing with her. Whatever she needs, I am 100% in!

I have been on some incredible and awakening retreats where the healing has been profound. I have visions in the future of sitting there with Seren in Bali, sharing our hearts, going deep, doing the work. I am all in and take full responsibility if I messed up, so I will put in the work she needs me to do.

Karl and I have done everything we could possibly do, and we love her endlessly, but I see that she has had a very different childhood from her brother and sister. Often the children that need the most love, ask for it in the most unloving ways, and I feel that Karl and I missed this so much when she was younger. We were always looking for ways to 'fix' her instead of holding space for her energetic and different personality.

Spirited children can be the hardest to love, and no matter how hard we try as parents, I am sure there will be some sort of negative imprinting on them. I get it, though; it happened to me as well. I too was that kid. I was always different, and out of the box. I tried to morph myself into so many different people when all I needed to do was embrace me and love and accept myself. This is my legacy for my children, to teach them that they are enough, and perfect just as they are.

If Seren wants or needs to go on a healing path, I will be there with open arms when she is older to support her and do it with her, unpacking it all and working through it. She is the most resilient and sassiest kid I have met, and she may well blissfully glide through life, while Daisy and Flynn may need the support. We never know how things are going to pan out.

I want you to hold that in your heart too. Never forget the gift you are giving to your future lineage by doing the work and throwing yourself into it. My mother and father would never have done that, but it wasn't their time; it was for this generation. I have not had my mother in my life since I was a teenager. She blames me for everything. That would take another book to write. I know I did absolutely nothing wrong, but I was her mirror, and for that, she could never connect with me. I

> Let go of logic and know you are always being guided by the part of you that exists in the spiritual plane — you simply need to trust.

once read that if you dislike your child, you inherently dislike yourself. Your child is an expression of you. I firmly believe that our spirited children trigger us as they are our biggest reflections. All that we dislike about them is often what we dislike about ourselves. Can you see that when we start to learn to love ourselves unconditionally, the triggers with our children become less and less?

Taking on Your Parents' Wounds

My mother was unable to take any of the blame for her behaviour or her life. My dad is starting to appreciate that what I went through as a child had a significant impact on my adult mental health. However, we recently had a falling out as me writing this book triggered him. He felt I was blaming my childhood and not taking any responsibly for my actions. I explained it wasn't about that, and I knew his reaction was just his ego trying to protect him. It doesn't matter how I got here; no one is to blame, and everyone was doing the best they could with what they had. I don't blame anyone and look at everything as a lesson. I believe I chose this life because there were lessons that I needed to endure. I trust everything, even the bad stuff. It's all been in my life for a reason.

I explained to my dad that I wasn't blaming anyone, I simply wanted to work on my healing, do the work, and become at peace so I could be a better mother. He softened and started to understand. My dad, at times, can be a narcissist, but on the flip side, he is also an awesome human and has been so supportive of my decisions in life, especially us moving to Australia. He has always been there for me, and we have only had a handle of fallouts in our life. Even though my dad says he didn't have any issues in his childhood, if we think bigger than this picture and allow ourselves to have a bird's-eye view of his life, I see it differently.

My dad was diagnosed with bipolar disorder around the age of fifty, and he still says to this day, the diagnosis was one of the best things that ever happened to him. He was finally able to understand and appreciate why he had suffered with his mental health for most of his adult life. Many experts believe that mental health disorders such as ADHD, bipolar and narcissism are developed through unhealed and unprocessed pain, whether that is theirs or simply epigenetics. I feel this is why it's imperative to begin this work, so we stop the pain from travelling down to future generations.

My grandma lived through the end of a war, and her mother lived through a war and losing her son, Geoffrey, who was a fighter pilot. I can't even imagine that pain in her heart. There was also alcoholism in the family, so even if my dad thought he had no problems in his childhood, there were emotions, pain, and suffering that were at play without him even knowing. Instead of looking at others with unkindness, we need to soften and allow our hearts to see them. There is pain there, even if those people don't understand or want to witness it.

I have always wondered if my dad had unhealed wounds, and maybe that is the reason that he parented me with such control. Maybe my behaviour triggered him, and instead of sitting with those triggers, he used fear, and control to parent me. I too did this with Seren, but she is part of the new wave of children who simply will not be controlled. Sadly, we are now turning to medicine to control them instead of seeing that their spirited ways bring with them presents of deep healing and inner wisdom. I believe there is a change in consciousness on our planet right now, and we are waking up from the deepest sleep. Generations of parents were not able to be conscious. It perhaps wasn't their time do the work, but we are bravely and gallantly stepping forward to wake up the collective.

Pain Holds the Key to Our Healing

When I think back to my PMDD diagnosis, I now see it as one of my biggest awakenings. I don't even remember how I started to wake up, to be honest. I think it found me. I think I was one of those souls reincarnated on earth, and I started to remember. As we begin to remember, sit with the pain, dig deeper, and unearth all that has been buried, we begin to rise into who we were meant to be in this life. It isn't always pretty and is often messy, but so we rise, and it is a beautiful thing.

I had just started to going church, and even though I don't go anymore, as my spiritually has taken many different twists and turns, I am so grateful for that two-year season in my life. It was the first time that I started to learn about God. I began to learn about Jesus and lean into his lessons of love. He would talk about letting go of anger and resentment and that we need to forgive and not hold onto pain. I held onto a lot of rage and blame towards others, but I learned that toxicity was harming me more than it was hurting them. Shortly after Seren was diagnosed, we medicated her, and that came with anger and judgment from others. Their words and actions affected me deeply, but I see they were triggering me, as that was how I truly felt about myself. I loathed myself for not being able to parent Seren without experts and medications.

Bless the darkness and bless the suffering as it here where you will truly find your golden light, buried within your chalice of the womb.

That was never who I wanted to be, and I can see how their words triggered me. The triggers are the guides, and it was only after I started to learn from my pastor about love and forgiveness that I let go of the past.

I also had never allowed myself to feel into the emotions of neglect and loss from my mother. I only sent her love, compassion, and kindness, but I also hadn't allowed my inner child's pain to be felt and to honour her and love her for all that she lacked in emotional nurture and love. Feeling into this pain was one of the first stages of healing with PMDD. I started to sit with the pain. When the anger, rage, and emotions would begin to rear their ugly heads mid-cycle, instead of reacting, I would sit in guided meditations and cry deeply. It was there that those deep wounds started to heal. Honouring the emotions, allowing them to surface, and sitting with the pain was one of the ways I began to heal. I had been harbouring the pain for years inside of my womb, and here was my gift, another month to sit with this pain, honour the inner child, and release all that had been in my life as a child. The more I sat with her power, the more I released, and the more I sent myself true unconditional love, the more I healed.

The Healing Frenzies

I also started to have lots of different types of healing from many different healers. From pastors in the church, prayer groups, shamanic healing, past life regression, breathwork. I did it all. The reason I had to walk away from the church was out of deep love and respect. The teaching at church was based on the Bible only. For me, I wanted to explore other healing modalities and practises, but most of the things I loved or wanted to explore were shunned by the church.

I was told that my love of meditation, crystals, and reiki was a sign of the occult, but I just didn't believe it in my heart to be true. It didn't feel right to me to make me fear something that had worked for me for so many years. I realised soon after going to church that my values and beliefs were not the same as everyone in the church, and I was starting to feel like the 'naughty schoolgirl'. However, I loved everyone, especially the two pastors, and I very much enjoyed going to church on a Sunday. I was fascinated by understanding more about Christianity and was exploring everything about spirituality in the new chapter of my life. I also loved the community and how accepted Seren was at church. The kids' church gave me some hours of freedom on a Sunday morning, and for that, I was truly grateful.

One Sunday morning, I shared my testimony in church about how I came to God, and when I finished, there were women in the audience crying. I shared how my entire life I had been running, living in nineteen houses in different cities, towns, and even countries since I was born. Once again, I had a yearning to go back and live in the country in Wales, even though it took everything I had to emigrate—I just couldn't settle.

I desperately wanted to be living in the hills again, surrounded by trees and nature. Even over the last six years living in Australia, I still yearn for the country even though we have a beautiful life living near the ocean. I now see that was part of my wounded inner child and the reason I had never connected with her, honoured her, or allowed her to be seen. In doing this work, I was finally able to make peace with the part of myself that was always wanting to move. I was yearning to recreate the part of my childhood before everything changed, and years of different types of abuse began. We will be going deep into this work in Chapter 6.

After my talk in church, women came up to me and started to tell me similar stories. They too, had been running most of their life, they too struggled with their mental health, and they were now taking medication. It blew me away. But how could they be struggling? They followed Jesus, they believed in God, and they attended church. I was told from the day I started going to church that if you let Jesus into your life, you would be healed. How were they not healed? How were they struggling? They had been to church their entire life. I started to believe that if these women hadn't healed despite being devout Christians, maybe I would need something more too. I respect anyone for their beliefs and values, but for me, on my journey I felt so intuitively that there was more. I spoke to my pastor about it, and she suggested praying to God, so I did, and then miraculously more and more started to come my way that was outside of the church.

Connecting Through Prayer

I would pray and ask for guidance, and then began to connect with women who were holding full moon women's circles. My heart was pulled to this so deeply. I also started to meet and become friends with some incredible people—reiki and shamanic healers and breathwork teachers. The more I prayed, the more they came, so I trusted intuitively that this was my path, and I leaned into all that the universe brought me.

We were also discouraged from meditating at church, but meditation was something that helped me greatly. I have a deep love of meditation, and it has helped to heal me in ways I could not have imagined. Breathwork has helped to heal some of my deepest darkest wounds, and without those healing modalities, I wouldn't be where I am today.

While I got so much from the weekly sermons, prayers, and healing from my pastor, I could feel there was more I needed to do that wasn't congruent with the church. I needed to go to those places and discover all the knowledge that came through many different teachings. Sound healing, reiki, shamanic breathwork, angel cards, crystals, and meditation were the catalyst to my healing, which is why I am so passionate about bringing this work into my community and the world.

I feel that our world today needs a combination of all things to heal, awaken, and evolve. We need to understand there is a power far greater than us but honour each other's beliefs and paths, without fear. For me, this is God, but I also connect with the words and energy of source, universe, love, creator, higher power, cosmos and greater consciousness. It resides in the same place, which is love. We are all created from source. Every living thing on earth comes from source energy, and it is a miracle that we are here in the first place. I genuinely believe we can't do the work when we are living through fear-based stories, but when we truly align with love and understand that our higher self is always trying to pull us in that direction, we can begin to heal.

I needed to do this work. I needed to release the pain from my womb, and even though I didn't know how, I trusted the process. Everything that happens to us happens for a reason, positive or negative. It is the universe bringing us back to harmony and love. I want you to start to be aware of everything around and see it as a guide to help you on your healing path. When I began my first awakening in Byron Bay some years ago, I started to notice 11.11 on the clock all the time. I would then begin to see other numbers, such as 000, 111, 222, 333 and 444. I began to do research, and I learned those were angel numbers. They were my guides connecting with me and letting me know all was well, and I was on the right path.

Signs from The Universe

Other times, I would have vivid dreams, tingly teeth (yes, that one is weird, I know). I would hear certain songs on the radio or see certain birds and animals. The animal kingdom is always trying to communicate with us; nothing is an accident. In fact, only last night we saw the most beautiful owl in our garden tree. The children and I watched in absolute awe at this magnificent creature just looking down on us and making such beautiful sounds. I knew this was a sign and thanked the owl for coming to me. Owls bring forth wisdom and change, and I was so grateful from the gentle nudge that all is well, and I am on the right path. The last few days for me have been unbelievable. I have also been visited by a white cockatoo, had some vivid dreams, received potent messages from my angel cards, and have seen angel numbers everywhere. I feel I am truly connecting with my guides right now, and I know they bring messages for me. I want you to start trusting these signs too. Let go of logic and trust with all your heart.

I have been interested in signs from the universe for about ten years, and I have had some incredible things happen to me from dreams. Once I had a powerful dream about a castle that we lived in. I also dreamt I was pregnant. At the time we were living in a friend's apartment as the home we had rented had flooded. We extended our one-month holiday in Australia to three months. We had no place to come back to after the entire property was destroyed by a burst pipe in the attic. We decided we could either go back to the UK during one of the worst winters in history, or we could stay in Australia until our visa ran out. We chose the latter. It ended up being the most remarkable decision of our lives. It was from this place that we made a conscious decision to emigrate to Australia, and within four years and two more babies later, we made our dream come true. The message here is to try and see the gift within the situation. From the flood and having no home for six months we came to discover that our dream was to live in Australia.

We arrived back in the UK, and after staying with different family members for a matter of weeks, Karl, Seren, and I stayed at our friend's apartment. It was there that I had the profound dream and was so moved by it that I immediately started researching castles for rent. I mean, you've got to dream, right? At the time, Karl's business was beginning to do well, but it certainly wasn't enough to be able to afford to rent a castle. I felt this dream so profoundly in my body —it felt more like a prophecy. At the time we were living near Liverpool, but as I am originally from Wales, I started to look at rental properties in Wales. Surely, I would find this castle in Wales. Right?

I then discovered this fantastic house, and strangely enough, it was where I grew up. It was in a tiny little village called Hawarden on the edge of North Wales. It was an 1800-year-old house set in the country overlooking fields. It wasn't a castle, but it was undoubtedly the most picture-perfect postcard house I had ever seen. I was drawn to it straight away, and even though I had no idea how we would afford it, I arranged a viewing that day.

As soon as I arrived, I fell deeply in love with it. I called Karl and arranged to meet him there after work. There were so many things about it the house that reminded me of my dream. Afterwards, I went with Seren to the local farm shop café. Beautiful chickens were roaming everywhere, as well as little free-range piglets. As soon as we walked over to the animals, there I spotted it in all its glory—the castle from my dream!

Ok, it was a kid's climbing frame, but it was almost identical to the castle in my dream! I knew it was meant to be and asked Karl to come straight from work and check out the house. Karl has always welcomed my crazy ideas, and even though it stretched us, he felt the same as me. This house was the one. We both felt so strongly that we needed to live there and moved our entire life to a completely different part of the country—and all that came from a dream!

We signed the paperwork and moved in a matter of weeks. Just before moving in, I found out I was pregnant, so again my dream came true. Never underestimate the power of dreams, even the bad ones. They all have messages for us. I also use an online dream interpreter after each dream and often journal them. There is so much we still do not understand about dreams, but I have learned that mine guide in so many ways—even saving Karl's life once as I shared in my previous book. My dream that he died almost happened, but acting on the dream, and taking him to the hospital saved his life!

Even today, we don't understand where we go when we dream or how it even happens, but I believe we are connecting with our higher self, and if we follow our dreams, they can lead us to the most beautiful destinations our soul knows we need. We ended up having two glorious, amazing, and wondrous home-births in my dream house. Even today, the house remains with us as one of the most beautiful times in our lives. In addition to having two babies in that house, Karl grew his business to the point that he could sell it, which meant we could fulfil our dream to emigrate to Australia. I was able to go back home to Wales before we left the UK shores, and it was one of the most magical times in my life. Three and half years of bliss and all from a dream, so listen to these inner knowings, and be guided by them—always.

Healing the Ancestral Line

If you are like me and struggle with your periods in some way, I want you to know you have been chosen to clear the debris from your ancestral line. I want you to see the honour and magnitude of this gift and not look at it as suffering or dark-ness. As I have shared for almost 25 years, I struggled with my periods. The only time I didn't was when I was pregnant or breastfeeding. Those were the most beautiful times in my life. I felt very connected to the baby, to my body, and to myself. I would practise meditation and HypnoBirthing and would only allow myself to think of birth as positive. I would meditate on the birth being wondrous, amazing, and the baby being in the correct position. I would practise fear release meditations and only allow myself to be immersed in positive birthing stories.

Many of my fears were not my internal fears, but the fears others projected onto me. Women who had traumatic births would tell me their stories, not out of unkindness, but perhaps in telling our stories, we can release them. What I have learned is that you can get lost in the story until you aren't sure if the story is of the complete truth. As humans, we can add bits on to make the stories even more terrorising; it's what we do. I am sure that is how I have lived my life too, even if at times I haven't realised it. Then you have a medical world that unfortunately will put the fear of God onto your pregnancy.

Our whole existence is fed on lies, corruption, and fear—you only need to put on the news to realise that. This book is about taking you out of that cycle and helping you see that you can reprogram your brain. It has now been proven that we are able to change the neuroplasticity of our brains, and future-self journalling is one of the proven tools that can help you with that. You don't need to remain in the story of your past. You have a new story to tell, one that hasn't even been lived yet, and you have the power to make your happy ending. We really can change our future and create our abundance when we honour all that has been, feel it, heal it, and then let it go.

That is why it is so important we understand how much is held in our wombs. Our connection with spirit becomes stronger when we are menstruating as the veil is thinner. Each month there is an opportunity to clear the stones from our bowl of light—to clear not only our debris but that of each generation before us. I suffered for so long because I didn't have the understanding or to the tools to work on my healing. So, each month, I struggled and tried to outrun the pain, until eventually kicking and screaming, I went within.

I discovered over the last couple of years that when the veil is thinner, we must be super clear of which guides we want to connect with us to show us the light. If this is the first time you have come across this work, then I will give you some language I have learned that has always helped me to connect with the right guides. Now I want you to imagine for a second that you are going to throw a dinner party. You would only want to invite the people you wanted to spend time with. You wouldn't want to invite random people off the street to come to the dinner party, so it's the same when you do this work. When you connect with your guides, you only want to connect with the guides of the highest truth and compassion. Just like with the dinner party, you don't want any old Tom, Dick, or Harry coming along that you don't know. Before I hold a full-moon women's circle or do a meditation where I want to connect with my guides, I always begin by asking my guides with the highest truth and compassion to please provide me with guidance or be in the space with me.

I am only days away now from the period, and I always noticed that my moods changed. I can get cross about things that before wouldn't have bothered me, but now instead of being super critical about myself, I honour that side of me and go within.

Each morning, I do a grounding meditation which helps me to anchor into my light, so I don't have any energies connecting with me that aren't of the highest good. I notice the difference now through my writing. Last month, I wrote about two thousand words which weren't in my voice. They were angry words about global warming and women not loving themselves enough and therefore having breast enlargements, Botox, and fillers. It was filled with a strange energy, and as I read it back to Karl, I was able to see it wasn't me. The same thing also happened to me in Bali a few months ago when writing this book. Again, it went down an utterly different path. Thousands of words were coming onto the page with anger and hate about children being overmedicated, etc. A few days later, after my period, I read it back and wondered what on earth had happened. I even write it about in my future-self journalling diary reminding myself only to connect with the guides with the highest truth and compassion.

The Women in The Red Tents

I genuinely believe that as women it is a sacred time when we menstruate, but the masculine energy has superseded this gift and made is something of a mockery. We are so much more than that. In the older days, women lived together in tribes, and they would all menstruate together in the red tent. Don't you think that's interesting we can bleed at the same time? Whenever I have lived with friends in the past, or even holidayed with them, we have all bled together. There is a reason why we are not honouring that blessing, and it is because of society's incorrect viewpoint of 'hormonal women'. With the jokes and memes and the fact that we do not honour the process anymore, it's almost like it has become something to be ashamed of and to hide. Now more than ever, I see women talking on social media about their bleed, honouring their feelings and emotions, and I always feel like, 'Yes, girl. We need more of this'! Let's talk about this more and inspire our daughters to understand that there needs to be no shame around it! I talk my girls about this and even my son, Flynn. Now in our house, your period is something that is sacred and should never be shunned or looked at in a negative light.

When women were in tribes, they would all menstruate around the new moon. They would gather together and take their children into the red tent. They would leave their husbands and then cook, clean, wash and tend to their children together. It was a wondrous time of connection, community, and healing. The women would understand each other and even cry together. The very reason that we cry is to realise the pain from our cells. Crying is one of the most beautiful gifts to our spirit. In this space, we learn to release and let go. What a gift we are given every month.

Across the world, the red tents are coming back. I had the privilege of being in a red tent three years ago when I first began my awakening. There were twenty women who opened, shared, cried, healed, and loved upon each other. I can still remember the power of that time, and the women I connected with like it was yesterday. I experienced so much healing in that red tent and declared what was as on my heart which was to help women and children. I have been doing this work ever since. It was also during that time I met my friend Sammi, who to this day is one of the most incredible spiritual healers I have ever met. At the time, I was going to church and was struggling with being both new age and Christian. She held my hand and encouraged me to connect with God, to lean into Him and ask him for guidance. She was also the first person to teach me about angels, archangels, and my guides. I am truly grateful to Sammi for all the lessons and the support that she gave me.

I began to discover tracking my menstruation with the moon and started to learn and understand the moon circles. I found that the new moon is a wonderful time to plant the seeds of everything we want to call forth in our lives, and the full moon is a wondrous and potent time to renew our energy and let go of what no longer serves us. What a magical thing it is to be able to flow with the energy of the moon and release any heaviness from our womb. I was so inspired by the magic, the full moon, and her healing power that I held beautiful full moons women's circles each month. I would hold them with my gifted friend, Emma, who was a shaman and healer. We would head to the beach, or in the cooler months, we would hold them in beautiful spiritual places used for yoga and women's circles.

I would feel the energy of women sharing their fears, their hearts, and their heaviness. We would release together, some would cry and together, we would let go. Emma would always start with a drumming healing, and then we move into meditation that I would intuitively write each month.

We would close the circle with a burning ritual where we would write down anything we wanted to release, and together we would burn those thoughts in a fire under the moonlight. What a gift it was to share with other women. I would tend to be bleeding around this time, as would many of the other women, and again it was a powerful time to release and let go as a collective energy.

Embodying the Pain

Every month, instead of trying to run from my pain and conceal it, cancelling appointments, and hiding away, I would sit in a circle with other women and learn to shine the light on the shadows. Only months before I began holding the circles, my PMDD was so bad I was unable to function for the week running up to my period. I would have to cancel all plans, and as I explained before, I got to the point where for one week a month, I couldn't make any plans. The full moon curve would push me right out of my comfort zone. I didn't want to make eye contact with anyone, let alone hold the energy for twenty women, but what I came to learn was that it wasn't about me, and it wasn't about them. It was about the unity of us all healing each other.

My mantra became, *When I heal others, I heal myself.* That, for me, was one of the most potent mantras as that is what happened to me. We purged together, we released, and I genuinely believe this connection of women goes far beyond anything we can comprehend. There is a divine feminine code that we have yet to understand, but we must trust in this potent magic and power. When we heal each other, we not only heal ourselves, but we heal our families and our communities. Being in circle is one of the biggest gifts we can give this world.

It is said that when women come together in circle, a powerful ripple of healing, light, and energy is sent out to the world.

Many times, when I would be in the circle, I would hold my womb. It was something that felt so instinctive to me, that somehow there was a healing power that could come from the cosmos and enter my womb, releasing and clearing the debris for me and my future ancestral line. I urge anyone reading this book to start to understand the correlation between our wombs, our menstrual cycles, and the moon. It has been one of the greatest understanding and gifts I have ever given myself. I mainly tend to track my cycle with the full moon, but at times in the year, my periods will also change and track with the new moon. Both cycles give us a chance to evoke either a newness and call forth changes or let go of what no longer serves us. Sometimes we need to go into the fullness and expansion of the cycle; at other times we can be creative, and at yet at other times we should rest and recharge. Just like the moon, it is important to honour the moon with a loving caress. Once you start to work with your cycle and the ebbs and flows that she brings, you will begin to discover how your cycle and your womb can become a magical dance of flow and energy with the creator and the universe.

The Power of The Moon

Each moon has a powerful and potent lesson for us to discover, and I have also shared two powerful meditations in Chapter 10 that can be used around the full moon and new moon. For the full moon, you can use 'release the heaviness' or 'shedding our skin'. The full moon meditations are designed to allow you to release, let go, and connect with your womb to do the deep, healing womb work. You can also use the new moon meditation, 'manifesting moon time' to bring forth all you desire, again connecting with the wisdom and potency of the new moon. I have also included prayers to guide you lovingly to connect with this source of magic.

For anyone who has been struggling with their periods, I would recommend researching and finding someone local who works with the womb, through either shamanic or holotropic breathwork, or a womb massage therapist. For me, breathwork has been the key to unlocking all the ancestral trauma and my trauma that was buried deep within her grasp. Once I was able to access the healing each month and clear the debris, I was able to learn to love all the lessons and wisdom she brought. I learned to bow to the inner wisdom my womb held and discovered she was nothing to fear, as deep within she held beauty and magic.

CHAPTER 4

THE TRIGGERS ARE THE GUIDES.

Once I began to witness that the triggers were the guides, I started to work through my unhealed pain layer by layer. Instead of blaming others and becoming the victim, I was able to see the gift within the triggers. I allowed them to rise one by one, shedding and letting them go. Within this space, I learned to heal my heart and changed the course of my future lineage. Even though it is hard parenting a free spirit, I was able to see the jewel within the lessons and learn to parent with love.

It was only two years ago that I started to understand triggers. I had a fear of driving on the freeways, which had plagued me for a decade. This fear then morphed itself into a fear of all types of travel. I have touched upon this before, but what I discovered is the fear didn't come from me being caught up in the London bombs, having to use the tube the next day, or then having a panic attack on the freeway. *The fear came from a place deep within, and the circumstances brought the fear to the surface.*

There were millions of people who were also caught up in the London bombs that day, many who didn't make it, many who witnessed unbearable pain, disability, and suffering. Many like me were caught up with the fear and anxiety of that morning; most went back to work the next day and continued with their lives. I did not, and from that point, my life became a hazy year of anxiety and panic attacks. I was later diagnosed with PTSD, but honestly, I feel it was already there waiting to pop to the surface. It just happened that the London bombs and the after-effects brought it to the surface.

Like blowholes at the beach, you must have the right conditions for the waterhole to blow. Too little tide, and you will see nothing, even though it's bubbling beneath; exactly the right amount of seawater, and the water will blow furiously out of the blowhole. I believe that is what happened to me.

I had managed to learn to love flying and trains through hypnosis (yes, I feared these at one point too). I was now able to drive everywhere, but the minute I would even consider going on a freeway, my anxiety would kick in. In Perth, we are blessed with other routes to get to places, so for almost four years, that was my plan. I took freeways off my car navigation system and Google maps and happily lived my life that way. No one even knew of my fear because I concealed it so well. If ever we went somewhere or I had a girl's weekend away, somehow magically other women would always offer to drive. My method was foolproof, and it worked, but I had a deep inner knowing that if I was avoiding that part of my life, I was not allowing the light into another part of my life.

Remembering My Childhood

Finally, I decided to try something called Rapid Transformational Therapy (RTT). I had shared my PMDD story on YouTube (link in Chapter 10), and a hypnosis practitioner reached out to me and said she would be able to help me. We chatted about my PMDD, how this could cause anxiety and anger (not just normal anger but a rage that would come on me each month). She was the first person who told me about triggers. She asked, 'Who is it that triggers you the most'? And I replied that it was Seren, my spirited daughter. The therapist went on to tell me that Seren triggered me as it would have reminded my subconscious of a time in my childhood when I wasn't heard or seen. I told her about my upbringing, how my dad was very strict and parented me like the Victorians.

Every day as a child, I would hear things from his mouth like, 'Children should be seen and not heard', and 'If you do that again, you will get a mighty one' (pants down over the knee and smacked with a rubber-soled boat shoe). My father's way of parenting was through control and fear. If I feared him, he could control me. While that worked when I was a child, as soon as I became a teenager, I rebelled and left home as soon as I could.

When I was a child, I had a little cloth I called Gee-Gee. I'd had this piece of fabric since I was a baby. I can still see it now—the blue, white, and yellow vintage colours, the soft, smooth feeling of the material. I would roll it into a ball and squish it around the palm of my hand while smelling it and sucking my thumb—such a great soothing technique when I think about it. Gee-Gee was my sanctuary, my safety, and my home, yet my dad would use it as punishment against me. Not only would he take Gee-Gee from me, but he would also put me to bed and leave the door open with Gee-Gee hanging over the bannister. If I got out of bed or even touched Gee-Gee, I would risk getting another mighty one. I can still remember crying myself to sleep while saying 'Gee-Gee' and reaching out my hand.

What we say to our children and how we say it can have a lasting effect on their mental health.

My little daughter Daisy is my soft, sensitive child. At almost nine years old, she still sleeps with her teddy and takes him on sleepovers. Some people have told me that she is too old for a teddy, but what right do we have to decide that? When I ask Daisy what Teddy means to her, she replies, 'He makes me happy, Mama'. Why would I ever want to take away such a simple thing that can bring my child happiness? I felt a lot of shame around my Gee-Gee, and whenever friends would come over, I would quickly hide it. I am proud to say Daisy will happily take Teddy to sleepovers; for her, there is no shame around it. My other two children got rid of their teddies at age two, and although they still have them in their room, they are confident without them. Daisy needs that reassurance, and I couldn't think of anything worse than taking away that comfort, even if she spoke out to me or did something wrong. We are all just figuring out life and configuring our boundaries, but I don't believe that fear and control is the way. However, I am not perfect, and I am not saying I have never used that type of parenting. I have, of course, but I am trying harder each day to be the mother I would have loved to have.

When I look back now, I can start to see the scars that were already forming. Shame, fear, control, and embarrassment—all these big emotions were already beginning to bubble up to the surface. The sad thing is, I don't really remember my mother being a big part of my life. It was mainly my dad who parented me. He was a great dad, too, very loving, caring, and providing, and he taught me everything. He taught me how to swim, how to tell the time, and how to ride my bike. He took me out shopping, and he would buy me clothes, shoes—even my first bra. Despite his strictness, he was a great dad and still is today. Even though we live 9000 miles apart, he calls me most days to see how I am, which warms my heart.

When Families Get Triggered

As I shared before, my dad and I recently exchanged some angry words, and it's funny that it was Seren who triggered him. As I mentioned before, my dad and I have only fallen out a handful of times, so for us to fall out is very, very rare. Seren was staying with him and my step-mum for a couple of weeks in the UK, and I was so grateful to them for looking after her and letting her stay with them. One evening she pushed some boundaries (as 12-year-olds-do), and instantly my dad went into control and fear mode. I wasn't there, but from what Seren told me, it was just like when I was a child, but obviously without the mighty ones. Most of us don't mean to be unkind with our children; we feel we are just doing our best, keeping them in line, and after all, it didn't do us any harm, right?

But we only need to look at the record levels of mental health issues now in adults. People don't believe in themselves; they have low self-esteem, they don't feel good enough, and many experts are now able to understand that these issues track back to childhood.

The crazy thing is that most of our parents aren't awake; they are still in the deepest of sleeps and don't understand what we are talking about. They don't understand it when we talk about the inner child, the mother and father wounds and healing. They can look at this as selfish and yet, for us, we know that doing this work is one of the most profound things to do in our lives. We are not only healing ourselves but stopping the generational curse in its tracks!

We should try to not show blame, ridicule, or anger to our parents. They were only trying to do their best with the level of parenting guidance they had. They were simply parenting us like they were parented, and fear and control was extremely prevalent back then. A good clip around the ear, some unkind words about how they would never amount to anything and sent to their bedroom without dinner. But how can this possibly instil love and kindness into a child's heart? For many children, the answer is that it can't.

Don't get me wrong. Children need boundaries, and when they cross them, there can be consequences. I get it; that is how I sometimes parent too, but anger, condemning, control, fear, and unkindness can be some of the worst parenting practises that we can possibly do. I am not perfect. I mess up, I fall into the trap at times too, but now I can notice it, move through it, and change the course of my parenting from fear back to love.

Using My Triggers to Guide Me

Seren is my trigger child, although I like to hope that she chose this karmic contract before she arrived here and chose me to be her mama. Sometimes I still react in the same way that my dad reacted with me, who I am sure triggered my Grandma when he was a child. I feel this has also played out on my mother's side too. I have never had a close relationship with my mother, and I have always felt that for some reason, she didn't like me. She would tell me constantly as a child; 'Susy, I love you, but I don't like you". I never quite understood why, but I do know that her words had a lasting effect on the way I felt about myself. I never liked myself, and I wonder if it was the initial imprinting from an early age of my mother's words. Furthermore, my nana didn't like my mum. My nana was so lovely to me, and I only have beautiful fond memories of her. She was such a lovely person, and I would cry when I would leave her house after the weekend. But my mother would tell me that my nana never liked her. She said even as a child, her mother would be kind to her brother and sister, yet never her. I wonder how far up the ancestral line this mother and daughter separation existed? I knew that I had to break this generational curse with my daughter, and even though she's my wild one and keeps me on my toes, I will never stop showing her abundant love and acceptance.

> We will keep repeating patterns until someone is ready to become conscious of the pain and brokenness; heal it and then change the course of the future lineage.

Being conscious of it, working through it, upping your parenting game, apologising, talking to your child, explaining it to them and deeply loving them will always prevail at the end of the day. We are only human. We are not perfect, and we are all trying our best.

Let us learn from each other, let us welcome the triggers as guides which will take us to the places that need healing and instead meet ourselves with love. When the practitioner told me about triggering, I was finally able to see them with compassion, finesse, and love. They still happened, in fact, all the time, but each time I would begin to go within and learn from it. I even found myself saying some unkind things to Seren the other day; you know, the usual. Maybe we have all heard these or said them in our lives: *Why do you always act like this? Why is there always fighting when you are around? Why do you cause trouble like this with your brother and sister?* I saw Seren's face, and I felt awful. When we arrived home from our day trip, I hugged Seren and apologised. I told her it was unkind of me to say those things, and I deeply regretted it. She told me it hurt her, and I said it wasn't true, I was just triggered, and I was sorry. The next day while we were walking along together by the beach, I told her about the bowl of light story that I shared with you at the beginning of the book. I explained that things people say to us, including friends and parents, can impact our light, and we should learn to shake these off.

I genuinely believe if we can keep continually working on ourselves, allowing the triggers to guide us to keep talking and communicating with our children, we will be walking in the direction of the light. I listened to a sermon today by a bishop on Oprah's podcast, and he talked about how the impact of our parents has a lasting effect on us. He said if we want to change our children, we need to work on ourselves first and foremost. He spoke of the light and magic within us, and how it sits at the very core of our existence. The bishop talked about an apple and explained that to get to our core, we need to remove the skin and the meat first to get to the seed. Once we find the core and our gift, we are able from the seeds to grow orchards and grow into the best versions of ourselves. He went onto say that most people get to the seed by rotting, addiction, prison, neglect or having a challenging miserable and difficult life before reaching their core and realising the gift within.

The bishop shared how we need not to wait until we rot to get to the seeds but cut through the core. Let go of all the pain, guilt, trauma, suffering, or being parented by wounded parents. He said we need to let that go and shine! That is what I have been doing over the last few years, and it truly has been the most amazing and awakening time of my life. Yet, somehow, I feel this is only the beginning.

The Lessons in The Triggers

When I look back on my breakdown, from the outside, my life certainly didn't look that bad. I wasn't addicted to drugs; I hadn't been to prison. I was married to my soulmate with three beautiful children, and we had just emigrated to Australia and were living near to the beach. My life looked amazing, but inside my head, it was a different story. I hated and loathed myself. I felt like I would never amount to anything, even though on paper, it looked like I 'd achieved a lot. My suffering was in my mind, and it kept me hostage for most of the month. I was able to fake it for about three weeks out of the month, but as I explained in the previous chapter, my menstruation would trigger me deeply. Not only would my moon time shine the light on the shadows, but my eldest daughter would trigger me so much. Every month it was like speed trigger work! It was an intense time, but I am deeply grateful for all the triggers, all the healing, and all the changes that came from that time in my life.

I want you to think about the people who trigger you and use your *Heal The Mother Journal* to answer these questions. Is it your parents, a certain friend or friends, your partner, your children? Knowing who triggers you and sitting with that and becoming conscious of it is the very beginning of your transformation. Instead of feeling angry at the person for triggering you, try and see it as a gift. Each time you get triggered, go within and find the root of the trigger. For me, it was the way I had been parented. It brought so much up to the surface and working on my inner child has been key to healing my triggers. We will be doing this work in Chapter 6 when we begin to work on the inner child. Even if you have done it before, it's essential to do the work again. It's such a big part of the healing work.

I wonder how my life would have played out if I knew about this work earlier? When I look back and see moments in my life, where I have been deeply triggered and had fallings out with people, I can now see it was, in fact, trigger work at play.

That mask we have over our eyes, the role we play out in society, to our friends, even our families, and ourselves is revealed when we are triggered. That is the part of us that can become angry, upset, jealous, fearful, spiteful, controlling, belittling, and unkind.

I genuinely believe that if we go deeper, we can discover so much about ourselves, for example, the part that wasn't seen or heard as a child, and that is why we get so triggered by certain people in our lives. However, they are in our life for a reason, and we should trust in the universe and the people who walk on our paths with us. Nothing is an accident. Only yesterday I was triggered by someone and to be honest, I can see that it had nothing to do with them. They are just living their life, and yet how they portray themselves triggers me. In the past, I may have made a remark to Karl that may have been belittling them in some way, as that's what we do in society, right? We gossip, and in some strange way, it makes us feel better about ourselves, especially when another person engages in the gossip with us.

However, learning about triggers makes me see that one of my core wounds is that I worry I am not a good enough mum. I know it isn't true, and it's taken me years to get to this point, but it's often still there, even now the voice is so small. Having the mother that I did always plagued me. I thought I would turn out the same as she did, and for me, that would be the worst thing ever. So, when I see others who seem to glide through parenting and make it look so easy, polished, and perfect, I can be triggered. Mothering is my greatest joy, but for me, it is messy, loud, unpolished, and far from perfect. But my kids are happy, and Karl and I are still living in love after twenty years together. I am proud of us and deeply love our little family.

Accepting Myself as A Mum

I am never going to be the mum with the perfectly manicured children or the mum who remembers everything. There is always someone who's lost their shoes, their coat or their school bag, but I feel each year, I am getting more organised, remembering more and upping my game. For some mums, this comes so easily, but I am learning that's because of who they are as people. Nobody is better than another person; we are all trying our best to figure things out. I am more of a slapdash, flying by the seat of my pants, relying on the universe to have my back and totally winging it most days kind of mum. I guess sometimes I wish I could be like the other mums. But I have learned to accept and love all parts of my parenting, and me doing the work and changing generational patterns is no easy task, right sisters?

When I feel triggered now, I can lovingly see it stems from my childhood and my inner child. I say only kind things about other mums and love and accept them for all their amazingness. I don't think unkind things through jealousy or lack. I simply go within and see that it's my trigger and has nothing to do with them. What a gift to able to turn that trigger around, acknowledge it, feel it and then release it.

How sad we have become in our western society that we are not taught how to feel in this way. We are not taught that triggers are there to teach others, and when others trigger us, they are merely mirroring our hidden and inner pain. In fact, our society has now made a mockery of unleashed pain and triggers. Reality shows such as *Big Brother* have become so explosive because you have a group of wounded individuals who are all being triggered by each other.

They trigger each other and bring out the deepest wounds and hidden trauma. It shoots out of people like poison from a venomous snake, and yet still people are unable to understand it.

I want to share with you a story about a TV star who was featured in the UK years ago, as I feel her story explains triggering perfectly. Triggers left untouched can cause immense pain and suffering. They can take us down dark paths as once the poison has been injected, it is tough to go back and remove it. Marriages have ended, relationships have broken down, friendships have been lost, and families have been torn apart, simply because people don't understand about triggers.

The Big Brother Race War

During the first few seasons of the highly successful reality TV show, *Big Brother*, they had a contestant called Jade Goody, who sadly passed away ten years ago. Jade didn't win the show, but she became the nation's sweetheart with her rags to riches phenomenon. Jade was raised in one of London's most disadvantaged communities and was raised by her single mum. When Jade was five years old, her mum had a motorbike accident and was no longer able to use her right arm. Because she was unable to work or look after herself and her daughter, Jade become a full-time caregiver to her mum at age five. She'd been estranged from her father and had witnessed many difficult things in her childhood, from drugs to prostitution. Despite her outlandish and brash ways, Jade had a beautiful heart, and the nation loved her.

As soon as she left the *Big Brother* house, she shot to fame overnight. The public loved her. She was on every magazine and newspaper cover, had a clothing line, perfumes, TV shows, and she also released her autobiography—all by the age of just 23. She was the first celebrity to become famous for simply being herself. She was loud-mouthed, full of fun, and shared everything and anything about her life, which is why the nation loved her. She got herself a handsome young boyfriend and shortly afterwards had two beautiful sons. Life was looking amazing for Jade, and it seemed everything she touched turned to gold.

She was at the peak of her career and only 25 years old when she decided to go back into the house for a new series of *Celebrity Big Brother* with her new boyfriend and her mum. Jade had a hard upbringing; both her mum and dad were drug addicts, and although her mum was now clean, she openly shared how much guilt she felt for Jade's childhood. Jade was from a town in London called Bermondsey. Jade was mixed-race as her father was black, and many of her friends were either black or mixed race.

Celebrity Big Brother is a TV series where celebrities from all walks of life and countries come together for two weeks in a house while being filmed 24/7. In this particular series, there were some well-known names—Jermaine Jackson, Leo Sayer, Dirk Benedict ('Face' from *The A-Team*), and some well known singers and actresses, as well as someone who was not well known in the UK but was hugely famous in India as a model, Bollywood actress and entrepreneur, Shilpa Shetty.

Shilpa was beautiful, successful, and loved by her nation. She told the other people in the house stories about how she has servants and bodyguards and how she had always lived that way. Her life sounded like that of a princess, and she was draped in the most beautiful and expensive Indian saris.

Jade and two other girls began talking about Shilpa behind her back, but the cameras obviously captured it. Hence, the nation was able to watch the drama unfold. They would snigger, say unkind things, and make fun of her clothing and her looks, yet I look back now and see that it was their egos at play and how they were being triggered by Shilpa. She was just being herself. She wasn't rude or unkind, but deep down, I think they all liked the idea of living like a princess in a palace. There is something enchanting about that idea.

When we understand that what we see and admire in others is often what we would love for ourselves, we can become more empathetic towards others. To be observant of that and to be inspired by others is the way for us to see all that is possible is within our grasp too. Anything we think about, dream about, and work towards is possible. I have seen and discovered that in my own life, namely that what we think about, we attract—good or bad. But the girls on the show were all young, and their egos played out from their childhoods, which were unkind, judgmental, and bullying.

Instead of complementing Shipla, they took it upon themselves to belittle her. Doing that is often all we know. We haven't transcended from the school playgrounds, and even in adulthood, we can show judgment and toxicity towards others. One of the greatest lessons I have learned is that it's not the other person's fault; only something deeper going on inside ourselves.

One night, Jade and Shilpa had a huge row. Jade lost it and started screaming at Shilpa. She said unkind comments about her race, her name, and her country. Nobody defended Shilpa, and the two other girls just looked on and laughed. It was very uncomfortable to watch, and thousands of viewers called in to complain.

It was a vicious racist attack, and the show producers had no choice other than to call Jade to the diary room and evict her. When the host interviewed Jade, she was so shocked. Jade said she felt disgusted in herself when she watched the footage, and she burst into tears. Jade explained she had apologised to Shilpa the next day, but it was too little, too late. The viewers had made up their minds. Jade explained that she was not racist and that so many of her friends were different races. She told the host, 'I am mixed-race, and my dad was black.' Call me anything, but please know I am not a racist'.

Others may disagree with me, but what I saw is that Jade was simply triggered by Shilpa. Even though Jade may not have understood or even accepted that about herself, she would have loved Shilpa's life growing up.

Living Like A Princess

Shilpa lived like a princess and grew up in a home that resembled a palace where she could have everything and anything she could have imagined. She had servants seeing to every need and desire, even dressing her. Jade had looked after her mother from the age of five. She had to do the cooking and even wash and clothe her mother. What Shilpa may have been was what Jade's inner child craved, which was love, security, and idyllic childhood.

I have created the life I desired and wished for during my whole childhood. All I ever wanted was to be a mum and have a loving, happy home, and I have succeeded in creating that, yet sometimes there is still a yearning for the childhood I never had. I used to feel I needed to 'get over it'. Karl would tell me to stop going on about it, and I felt ashamed for harbouring those feelings and sadness. But doing the work on my inner child, allowing my triggers to heal me, and acknowledging my pain and sadness has been key to me at last living a peaceful, happy life. For the first time in my life, I have no desire to contact my birth mother ever again. I am not the beaten-down child anymore who keeps wanting to go back. I have finally made peace with it all and have accepted that she will never be in my life, but I am truly grateful to her for giving me life.

I have been married to Karl for almost fourteen years, and we've been together for twenty. I always wanted three children and desperately wanted to move to Australia and live by the ocean. I have been able to create all that through the law of attraction and always following my dreams, but I struggled for most of my adult life to accept my childhood. I have been so blessed. I have not been raised on a refugee camp, and I had endless love from my grandparents, yet there was so much missing from my mother, and even from my father whom I very rarely saw as he worked so much. Don't get me wrong; I am deeply grateful for his commitment. He did what he had to do, but his internal compass was all about success. If he looked successful on the outside, he would feel it on the inside, but we all know that that doesn't play out to be true, and that's why so many successful and wealthy people are miserable. Money doesn't always make you happy.

Why does our childhood affect us so much even when we have carved out the life that we desired? We haven't carried on the generational curse, and we have changed significantly from our families, why does that feeling of low self-worth reside within?

We are living 95% of our lives in our subconscious mind, and we understand now that our subconscious mind is based on our pre-programming. Think of yourself as a hard drive. All the pre-programming from our childhood—school, parents, grandparents, and our peers—is hardwired into that drive, so bullying, feelings of inadequacy, unkindness, belittling, and a feeling of not being seen or heard as a child forms part of our subconscious.

Changing Our Inner Programming

We were always led to believe we couldn't change that hard drive, and once it was in, that was it; there was no changing it. We now have information and understanding that we can change the brain's neuroplasticity and therefore change our inner negative beliefs, pain, and suffering.

I have been able to do this in my own life over the last few years, and I know it is possible for you. I was haphazardly trying everything, so I have included in this book all the things that have worked for me. My intention is to give you a healing roadmap by giving you the correct information, tools, and guidance. It's essential to mention that healing never stops. It's an on-going journey which helps us to transcend and come back to love of ourselves and others around us.

I believe my programming was a tape that was playing over and over that I wasn't worthy of love. I wasn't enough that my mother and father would want to spend time with me. I endured different types of abuse from some family members, and that reinforced my feeling that I wasn't worthy. I remember spending a lot of time at both my grandparents' and my nana's house. As I mentioned before, I can recall crying deeply every time I had to leave my nana's house. My grandparents' homes become my safety and my sanctuary. The thing they gave me was love, safety, kindness, and time, which is something I didn't have at home. As I became a teenager, I would spend a lot of time at my friends' houses; they always felt safer than at my own house. I loved the family feeling I felt at my friends' houses. I once spent the entire summer holiday living at a friend's house, and that still gives me some of the happiest memories of a summer well spent.

There was so much love, laughter and togetherness that I didn't get at home. While from the outside, my life may have looked fantastic—a big house by the sea, a stay-at-home mother, and a father who was the local bank manager in our small Welsh town, inside it was a living nightmare.

I look back now and wonder how my mother managed to raise me when she was an alcoholic. I had a blended family as well, with a half brother and sister from my mother's first marriage. My brother and sister both had issues, and my dad always said they had seen 'too much' before he met them at the ages of twelve and fourteen. He adopted them just before he married my mother, and then I was born the following year. I do always remember my mother saying I was made through love and was very much wanted, which gives me comfort.

I had a wonderful extended family of aunties, uncles, and cousins and my earlier days until around the age of eight were beautiful. I remember long, hot summer days staying at my cousin's house, or staying with friends and grandparents. Even though I saw both my sister and brother kicked out of home at the sweet age of sixteen, and there was a lot of fighting, I still have some fond memories. I don't ever remember being close to my mum. As hard as I try, I can't remember much love there. I do believe she tried, but I guess her true passion was helping other people, which is why she became a local councillor. When your biggest desires are helping save the world and a love affair with whiskey, there isn't much time for anything else.

Listening to The Mean Girl Again

For as long as I can remember, I had a repetitive voice that would tell me I was a failure. It was relentless, my pre-programmed subconscious, and my inner mean girl. She was a stern voice that would get louder and louder around my menstruation time. Understanding my subconscious and my childhood has been key to me knowing my triggers. While having a session of Rapid Transformational Therapy, my mind took me to some childhood memories that I believe were affecting me in my adult life.

During hypnosis, my mind took me back to memories when I was left in the back of the car at night while my parents drank in the pub. I could remember it as clear as day. They made a bed for me in the back of the car, put my pyjamas on, gave me a pillow and a duvet, and went into the pub to drink. My dad swears it was only the once, but for me, I feel it happened more than that. Maybe it didn't, but the memory is deeply ingrained into me. I always had a feeling my parents didn't want to spend time with me, that I was somehow in the way of their lives. I always remember from a very early age feeling as if I was simply in the way.

My dad, as I have shared before, was a bank manager, but he also had a shoe repair business and was the landlord for bedsits and flats. At the same time, we lived an old house he was renovating. When I look back with all my adult understanding, I see he was simply running from himself. We don't all need to be alcoholics or addicts to run from our internal suffering; workaholics are doing it too. It's too painful to sit with where we have been or who we have been, so instead, we run through life.

I was that person too. I was running through life at a million miles an hour, somehow hoping that by doing that, I could raise happy, healthy children. I discovered it was not possible as monkeys do as monkeys see. If I am stressed, anxious, and worn-out, it will filter through to my children. It can also morph itself in different ways. Children may struggle to sleep, get up in the mornings, have friendship issues, anger issues, or distraction issues at school. Sadly, there is a distinct lack of looking at the family before we so rapidly diagnose kids, and from my own experience often with a diagnosis comes medication. What I discovered at our home is that when I am happy, my kids are happy, and our home is happy. It really does begin and end with me.

> The old paradigm teaches us that we must work harder and faster than the next person. The new paradigm teaches us that all we need is in the present moment, and to sit with that is one of the greatest gifts we can give ourselves and our children.

After my dad and I recently had a small falling out, I have been using my time to go within and discover why I was so triggered by my dad when he was strict with Seren. Within minutes of hearing Seren upset, I began to cry. I felt her pain as my own and immediately went into a knee jerk reaction and called my dad. Even though we only exchanged a few words to each other, we both jumped straight into our egos. We will talk more about egos in Chapter 8, as understanding our ego will help us not only to identify how it helps us at times but also how it can stop us from truly growing from our heartfelt purpose.

Understanding the Pain Body

My dad and I immediately went into our egos, and as Eckhart Tolle explains, he looks at the ego as a pain body. When I first learned this concept from his book, *The Power of Now: A Guide to Spiritual Enlightenment*, my whole twenties began to make sense within an instant. I met Karl when I was 23 years old, and for the first year, our relationship was idyllic. I was convinced we would be a couple who married early and had babies straight away. That was my dream, and from the age of 24, I was unbelievably broody. I was so desperate at some point to get married and have a baby, and after finding my Prince Charming, I felt it was inevitable it would happen.

But as Eckhart explains, we can keep our pain body hidden, often even denying part of ourselves, hoping and praying somehow it has gone. He shares that when partners move in with each other, they somehow relax a bit, and then the pain body is shown. We hear about how relationships can change when we get more comfortable with each other. Karl and I didn't move in with each other until we had been dating for two years, but my pain body started to rear its head after twelve months. I remember one night when Karl and were sitting and talking, and he shared how I wasn't like other girls, how our relationship seemed perfect, and how we both knew that we were 'the one'. Only weeks later, during our first big argument, my pain-body snuck up from the depths and my anger, insecurity, and venom came out in full force. I was full of neediness and was constantly feeling and worrying that we were drifting. I thought I wasn't enough for Karl, and the more I worried, the more my pain body came out in full force.

Karl too had a pain body which began at the age of eleven. He remembers the day his dad left home, making a conscious decision that he would work hard, wear a suit, and be successful. He also made a promise to himself that he would support his mum after his dad left his mum and three children to fend for themselves. Years later, Karl asked his dad for some money to go towards new a new bike. When his dad said no, he made a promise to himself never to ask anyone for anything again. Karl never let his feelings about his parents' divorce come to the surface. He would never acknowledge them or talk about them, and he simply repressed them, further growing his pain body. Karl had a very negative view of marriage and children. When my pain body started to show itself, it was met by Karl's, who reaffirmed that relationships, marriage, and children were a negative thing.

Karl was that guy who was very comfortable being on his own. He liked his own time, and he never relied on anyone. These traits have made him very successful in life. In the last year as he was going through his awakening, Karl finally realised that he acted the way he did after making that conscious decision at the age of eleven never to need anyone, ever.

So, there you have two very different pain bodies—one which felt unloved and unworthy, and the other which would be triggered around arguments, fallings out, and commitments. However, after four amazing years together and at the age of 28, I was now ready for the next stage. I talked a lot about marriage and children, but Karl didn't want to get married and have children until much later in life, maybe in his mid-thirties, and I didn't want to wait. So even though we were deeply in love, we started to argue a lot, and in the end, decided to split up and go our separate ways.

Eckhart Tolle feels strongly that we have bigger pain bodies when our parents have gone through trauma, or if we have experienced trauma as a child. He believes that the pain body, or entity as he calls it, can even be there when we are born. He shared how he feels he was born with a pain body, and that led to him feeling depressed and suicidal as a child. It took for him to experience the death of his ego to be finally free from his pain-body. Eckhart believes that when we are exposed to our parents fighting and arguing all the time, that increases the size of our pain bodies. Whether we call it pain body, entity, or trauma, it can dramatically alter our mental health and our resistance to life's normal ebbs and flows. It can affect our relationships with others, including our children, and even our relationship with ourselves.

Soul Mates Destined to Be Together

When I reflect on my earlier relationship with Karl, I wonder how things would have played out of we had the tools and understanding to manage this chapter in our life—if we had been awake to our suffering and pain bodies and if we had healed together. We were so lucky; we made it through. I feel so many don't even when they truly love each other. Karl and I both feel we are soul mates, twin flames destined to be here on earth together in this time. I am grateful our love and commitment to each other was strong enough to withstand the storm. There were times when I didn't believe we would make it. Letting go of ego, understanding childhood trauma, and being able to work through our healing has saved our beautiful love and has given our children the family we never had in our childhoods. Karl still triggers me, as I do him, but now both of us can see past the trigger and understand it is something held deep within. When we get triggered by Seren or others, we can help and support each other through this. We can hold space for each other and consciously navigate our relationship.

From now on, be aware of your triggers. Use your *Heal The Mother Journal*, shine the light on these shadows, and use future-self journalling to work through this part of your healing journey. Think about the people who trigger you and go deeper. Use the Triggers Are The Guides meditation, which you can find in Chapter 10, and start to unpack why you are triggered by these people. Often, you will discover that it stems from your childhood. Your inner child is the child who needs loving and reparenting, and all this is within your grasp. I want you to let go of anything that has gone before, mistakes you feel you have made, and allow yourself to hold the vision of the person your higher self guided you here to be. Rise up, buttercup. You are everything you imagine you can be.

> Instead of seeing the triggers as problems in each other or the relationship, you can learn to shine the light within and allow the triggers to heal you.

Removing the Veil from My Eyes

Over the years, I have had some challenging relationships with others, from work colleagues to family members. Allowing myself to now look back on those moments, I can see that what was at play was a concoction of pain bodies, ego, and triggering! How easy life would have been if I had those tools. I genuinely believe the road to enlightenment is going through those painful lessons, walking through the fire, and allowing ourselves to discover the lessons and come out of the other side freer and more empowered.

I have held this in my heart for a long time and now never carry any guilt or regret—even who I have been, mistakes I had made in my life when I was younger, all the crazy lessons I endured. I don't hold anything towards them. I feel that one of the most incredible things I have learned is to honour what was and allow what will be to come forth with trust and reverence.

Eckhart Tolle tells us that the work of Jesus, one of the greatest teachers of love, was to let go of anger, resentment, and instead forgive others. He told us that by holding on to anger and resentment, it only hurts us, not the other person. Learning to use the relationships of others as a vessel to our healing is true ascension. You become lighter, you allow for more joy in your life, and you learn to let go and accept what is. In the next chapter, we are going to talk about boundaries, which is something I have discovered in the last twelve months, and I cannot explain to you how much my life has changed because of it. I have learned to put boundaries in for my children based on love, not fear-based projections. I have learned to put boundaries in with my marriage, my work, and my friends and family. I feel liberated, and my only regret is that I didn't know about this work before. As I have felt so deeply throughout this book, we get there when we are supposed to, and when we do, we must trust we are always divinely guided.

I have written half of this book while travelling along the east coast of Australia. Karl has been driving, and I have typed tens of thousands of words. Yesterday when I wrote all about pain body and what happened to Karl and me in our twenties, I stopped writing and shared with him what I'd written. We both got so emotional, as we now so clearly see what happened all those years ago. As I shared in this book, Karl went through a massive awakening last year. He shared publicly at *The Dairy of an ADHD Mum* book talk that he was only able to obtain a deep connection with our children and to some extent me when he began working on his healing. Karl had trapped emotions from his childhood and had kept them buried deep within, but in suppressing any negative feelings, he also suppressed joy and a deeper connection of love with others.

Letting Go of Our Parents' Wounds

During his awakening, Karl had a realisation about his dad, who at fourteen was orphaned and raised by his brothers, who weren't much older than him. His dad had no parents to guide and support him over those very crucial years. When he met Karl's mum just five years later, they fell deeply in love, married at twenty and then conceived Karl almost immediately. Eleven years and three children later, Karl's dad left their family home and never came back.

Karl realised during his awakening that not only was he carrying his wounds but also those of his father, and maybe even his grandfather. Through conscious and connected breathwork, we can release not only our suffering but that of sixteen generations before us, allowing this not to pass on to the next generation. Both Karl and I have spent the last twelve months attending many breathwork ceremonies, and I have also learned to become a breathwork teacher. As I had shared before, this allowed me to clear years of debris from my past, even from my experience in the womb, and go back through my mother's pain. During one deeply cathartic breathwork session, I was able to feel in my body that my mother didn't have a connection with her mother and that my nana also didn't have a deep loving connection with her mother. I was able to see and feel that my ancestral mother line had struggled to connect with their daughters. What a tremendous honour it was for me to witness that and to be able to stop the generational curse and change the course of history for our future daughters.

Karl's awakening came from a Christmas present I bought him, which was an eight-week shamanic men's course here in Perth. Although he did not want to go and insisted that I get my money back, the course changed his entire life. After we chatted yesterday, Karl shared with me how he'd feared marriage and children. I had to persuade him to have our third child, Flynn, and it's only been in the last year that he has finally allowed himself to see the gift of our three children. He always thought we should only have two children, but again he has a deep-rooted fear of children and marriage; he felt the more children, the more he would have his wings clipped and not be free.

I, on the other hand, have deeply yearned for another child since I had Flynn, who is now six years old. I have felt a deep desire to have another baby, and it has never left me. As I am writing this book, I think how beautiful it would be to have another child. Karl and I have both done so much work. We have healed some profoundly deep wounds. We have been plant-based, alcohol-free, and both been on such a profoundly immense spiritual path together (more of which I will share later in this book), that it would be beautiful to consciously create another baby.

I decided to talk to Karl after writing this chapter. I feel that for so long, I have kept these feelings suppressed, hoping that they might go away, but in fact, they have become louder. I have shared how this book was helping me so much just to write these words on the paper, and I know my words will help so many beautiful women who are ready and willing to do this work. I also understood why I had been so needy over the years, as when Karl would want to go on holidays of adventure by himself. I would feel in some way that he didn't want to be with me. It was all based on my childhood. Karl has now understood why he had a desire to have so much time alone, which again was deep-rooted from his childhood.

I know his heart and feel his deep desire for adventure and to experience the world, but my years of co-dependency towards Karl caused so many unnecessary arguments around his travels. I didn't want to be apart from him, and I couldn't understand how he wanted to be apart from me. However, my insecurity wasn't Karl's fault. It was all driven from my childhood, and when I was able to witness that, I softened and realised it was never about me. His wanting to travel alone didn't mean that he didn't love me; it simply meant that he was living out his dreams. Loving me and loving his dreams were not mutually exclusive. When we learn that our entire happiness comes from within, we can stop looking elsewhere to find it. When we stop trying to allow others to fill the void within us, we can heal the co-dependency we have may have placed upon our partners or others.

To be able to have done the work and continue to do the work together allows you to have a conscious relationship built on love, respect, and deeper cultivation of each other's heart and soul.

Wanting Another Baby

I want to share something very personal with you. This morning we decided to get up at 6 am to begin our last leg to Adelaide in the campervan. I had a bath before I went to bed last night and wept. Karl came in and asked me what was wrong, but I felt like I couldn't share my heart with him—the feeling and deep yearning for a baby that has never left me. I thought he would shun me, tell me there is no way we are having another baby, and then I would feel sad, and my heart would ache. For the last two weeks, I convinced myself I was pregnant. Some incredible things have happened, and I've some deep signs and an inner knowing that a baby boy is coming, but last night as I felt my period coming, I started to weep. I wondered how I'd been able to manifest so much in my life, yet here I was at 43 years old, and I had been unable to manifest another baby for the last seven years since Flynnie was born.

I would share with family, friends, and Karl that I would have loved another baby, but Karl has always been adamant it would never happen. I loved and respected him for that. I am so grateful for our three beautiful children, and I know that it is an honour not everyone has in this life. The reason I am sharing this with you is that it is part of the boundary work. This work goes so much deeper than telling people what we don't want. It's also about speaking our truth and telling people exactly what we do want. It's about honouring ourselves, doing the work, sitting with our truth, and then expressing it. I got to that point, and I felt my intuition say, *Tell Karl.*

So, the very next day, we both woke early to begin our very last road trip, and I knew in my heart this was the time to be honest with Karl and share my heart. As I shared my truth with him, I cried deeply, and I saw tears in his eyes too as he listened intently.

To my absolute amazement, Karl listened and cried with me. He shared how he wouldn't see another child as a bad thing anymore, and he also felt that we would have the most beautiful, awakened little soul. To be able to go through this journey as a conscious couple, to create a life consciously, to prepare my body, knowing that my energetic body is also healed, fills me with such joy. I know there is a separate book for you—for mothers, for daughters, for sons—a book that will completely change how we give birth and prepare our bodies for giving birth, and a book about conscious and connected, conception, pregnancy, and childbirth.

So, we held each other, cried deeply, and decided we would try for another baby. I cannot tell you how I feel as I write this to you. I can't believe the changes that have happened to our relationship in the last two weeks. Some serious magic has been woven into our lives. It all came as a result of our deep healing over the last two years, and my commitment to sharing my truth. This book now is truly going to be a labour of love. I can't wait to birth this book, knowing that by the time it is published and birthed out into the world, I could be carrying, growing, and creating my force of life within my womb. And just to think, this whole huge change in my life came from writing the chapter on triggers. Now, do you see how powerful these triggers are? When we are triggered by others, especially our partners, there is a deeper force at play. Only when we acknowledge the force, let it rise, allow it to teach us, heal us, and guide us can we truly find our light.

CHAPTER 5
BOUNDARIES ARE THE ANSWER YOU SEEK.

Many of us struggle with boundaries, and this can often come down to how we were parented. If we weren't raised with abundant love and self-assurance, that could often mean we are people pleasers. Being a people pleaser can drain your energy, affect your relationship with yourself, and cause anxiety within families. Children can feel they aren't important, as you constantly give to others, thus repeating the damage. Through boundary setting and honouring ourselves, it is possible to have a more conscious, meaningful life.

Old paradigm boundaries:

- Children should be seen and not heard
- You will do exactly as I say, or you will be punished
- You will respect your elders
- Children push boundaries to see what they can get away with
- My child always knows how to push my buttons

New paradigm boundaries:

- Children should be seen and heard
- Their defiance is simply a reflection of you—they are your mirror
- The lessons they bring are part of the paradigm shift
- Children push boundaries to heal us
- Your triggers are the gateway to your healing.

We are in a poignant time in history. For the last century, we have been parenting through control. Children have been subject to such tight boundaries that they have been unable to express themselves without fear, ridicule, or punishment. For so long I would hear elders say:

'We were not allowed to speak to our parents like that'.

'If we had spoken to our parents this way, we would have been spanked'.

'Children of today need a good hiding. Bring back the cane. It didn't do us any harm'!

It was not so long ago that children were given the cane in schools, and what was their crime? Speaking out against the teacher? Sharing their truth? Triggering the teacher's childhood pain and suffering?

That's what we did, right? If we were triggered, we would smack or beat the child? I am not perfect—far from it—and I have made many mistakes as a parent, but I cannot see how that is the answer.

Allowing Our Children to Be Seen and Heard

As you know, I was raised with anger and aggression. I was never allowed to speak out at my father, and if I did, I was smacked. What message does that give a child? Speak your truth, and you have pain inflicted upon you? I don't remember my mother being overly violent in a calculated way but more of a hazy, she'd lost her mind, drunk way. She would reach a certain point and would start smashing things—plates, crockery—which would all come tumbling down in the kitchen. Windows would be smashed, and sometimes the police would be called, and while it didn't happen very often, it's still etched in my memory.

It has been fascinating raising my three children, as it is my eldest daughter, Seren, who triggers me the most. I feel intuitively that this behaviour has happened in my lineage for a long time. No matter how hard it is, I will continue to break the generational curse and work on the triggers and boundaries. Seren is my spirited child, and this was prevalent at just the tender age of thirteen months. Biting, hitting, kicking other children and me—those first few years were a wild ride. Sometimes, I got it wrong. I hit her back (something I still regret), but these children don't come with a set of instructions and the way we were parented filters down to us. I was often advised that if a child bites you, then bite her back. However, that is again very much of the old paradigm and something I am moving away from as I try to raise my children consciously.

I have parented Daisy and Flynn in a completely different way—calmer, more loving, and with more compassion. So, why not Seren? One word—triggers. She was the child brought into my life to trigger me. It could have gone either way. I could have been continually triggered by her, played the victim parent role, cried, lost my shit, cried some more, told people how bad of a child she was and failed to see that in fact, her triggers were here to heal me. I am so glad that through this journey, I have learned the latter, and that is why I want to teach this work. It is so important. As a friend reminded me today, Seren is my mirror; that is why she is here.

> Society doesn't teach us that spirited children have that title for a reason. They have the spirit of what was intended for them woven into the very magic of who they are.

Childhood Imprinting

As children, we are imprinted by our parents and the people around us, and that happens until around the age of eight. Children's brains are like sponges; they are soaking it all up. I remember when I used to take Seren to many different baby classes. Baby massage, baby rhyme time, baby sensory—it all felt beautiful, and I enjoyed those days so much. I would spend the hour cooing and being attentive and loving to my baby, but who I was behind closed doors was far more critical to her genetic make-up than at the baby classes. My reactions, emotions, fears, and anxieties were the very things that would be imprinted onto Seren, not the mother and baby classes. They were lovely and helped with the mother/child bond, but it's the other 23 hours of the day that would create the person Seren was in this life. That is what counts that is the crucial work. As I have shared before, around 95% of what we do each day comes from the subconscious—that is when we are unconsciously thinking. That part of our brain is years of programming and imprinting from our parents and our childhood. Many of my fears, I have realised lately, are simply not even mine. My fear of freeway driving and fear of planes (although these have both been healed now), were my mother's fears, not mine. I was merely unconsciously living them out, not realising they were not mine. How many fears, emotions, or anxieties have you carried on from your mother? Spend a moment thinking about it, maybe even journalling it and see what you come up with.

When I look back at my triggers, I see that they were simply a part of me, as I couldn't express myself as a child. There was a wounded part of myself that hadn't been healed. That wounded inner child was still hurt, frightened, and unhappy. When Seren would do something and push the boundaries, she was simply pushing the wounded part of me that needed healing. Without knowing it, she was pressing the big red button of my inner pain.

The old paradigm is that children need boundaries, so they stay out of harm's way. There are instances when this is true, for example, not running across the road when there is a large wagon coming (yup, this was Seren at age six)! It can be scary as a mum, and we are wired to protect our children, but often boundaries can be created from our inner fears and insecurities. My story was that I wanted to be a good mum, I didn't want to parent as my mother parented me. There were no boundaries set by my mother; anything went. She would often not be home when I arrived home from school, even as a small child of about seven years old. My mother would drink and drive and would be drunk when I would come home from school. If we look at our boundaries as our values, it is easy to see how my mother had very little values on child safety.

Needing Safer Boundaries

Years later, around the age of ten or eleven, I was put in a potentially dangerous situation with an extended family member who had no boundaries when it came to his sexual expression of masturbation or watching pornography around children. I won't go too much into detail here, but what I will share is my parents didn't put any safe boundaries in place to protect me even when they discovered this was happening. I explained to them that nothing physical towards me had taken place, and my mother agreed that she would deal with it by threatening him with a baseball bat. As you can imagine, this didn't worry him too much, so the behaviour continued for many more years. I didn't have the tools to protect myself and ask him to stop. I wasn't taken out of the situation or given support or guidance to keep myself safe. Instead, I continued the pattern of freezing and would pretend to be asleep whilst it happened.

I am very lucky and forever grateful this type of abuse didn't progress any further. In some ways, I am thankful for the lessons—for understanding I need to keep my children safe by continually talking to my children about their boundaries when it comes to their bodies, continually empowering them about their bodies and having 'those talks' with them. I come from the generation that didn't talk about that stuff; we didn't even talk about sex or drugs. It all just got brushed under the carpet. I feel now more than ever at home and in schools we are educating children about boundaries, what feels safe, what doesn't feel right in their tummy, talking to them about their intuition, and listening and honouring it.

I have learned that one of the biggest ways to prevent abuse is by educating our children, empowering them, and giving them tools to speak their truth. We need to teach them to understand that they are love, and they deserve the most utmost respect. We must also keep working on our stuff, so we do not pass it onto our children. Just because something harmful happened to us does not mean it will happen to our children.

Years ago, I became paranoid that something could happen to my children. I remembered what had happened to me; my brain catastrophised it all. This is the part of us called the ego, and I will explain this more in Chapter 8. To heal means to be awake, and to be awake means we can differentiate between our ego and intuition. Our ego wants to keep us safe, and there have been times when we have really needed that, but I knew I was making boundaries based on fear of what had happened to me. I have learned to understand through spiritual practise that what happened to me happened for a reason.

Finding Forgiveness

It was during a spiritual healing that I was able to see clearly why this family member had been in my life. It became so clear to me that we had both chosen to be in this life together so we could teach each other the lesson of forgiveness. Each lifetime we have a chance to work through something before we go onto the next life. Understanding that felt congruent with my heart and gave me some sort of peace. This is not the case for everyone, but I have learned that the key to letting go and healing is forgiveness. I guess the biggest lesson for me from this experience was to not pass my imprinting onto my children. This was my experience and my story and shining the light on it, moving it through my body and healing it, has allowed me to not pass this fear on to my little family. Instead, I always talk to them about their boundaries with their body, and I will continue to keep empowering them in this way.

Many other things happened to me as a child, and it was always based on a lack of boundaries. When I think back, I realise how my mother allowed me to be in some potentially dangerous situations as a child and a teenager. While writing about this, I have found myself going through phases of anxiety, anger, and emotions. I wasn't aware this was linked to me going back to these memories. Silly things happened, like Karl triggering me because he wasn't helping around the house and Seren being her teenage self and being so strong-minded. But, having sat with all these feelings today, I realised it was the memories coming back up for me. I realised I hadn't allowed them to move through my body. If anything is coming up for you, please refer to Chapter 10, as I have given some information there for you on support with sexual trauma. I have also recorded a meditation to help you move through this chapter, and please use your *Healing The Mother Journal* to honour this part of you. I believe if we can shine the light on the shadows, honour what happened, try and find the lesson, and learn to forgive and move through this, we are honouring our healing.

I fully respect that not everyone feels the same, but this is my knowing. I have had past life regression before, and I have been able to see my past lives clearly. I was able to heal each life through past life regression, and then those things weren't prevalent in my life anymore. I have family members who are petrified of water for no reason, and I always wondered did something terrible happen to them in a previous life around water? However, many other people do not believe in this concept, which I completely respect. There is so much we do not understand about life and death, and I can only draw on my experiences.

> We must learn to let go of logic, fear, resentment, and suffering and allow our hearts to expand only to the vibration of love.

My Spiritual Children

My beautiful boy Flynn talks in an American accent and tells us in detail all about his previous life in America. He recently took Karl fishing and even though he had no experience on how to fish, he told Karl what to buy from the fishing shop with precise detail. When we talked to him about this, he told us that he used to go fishing with his dad Steve when he lived in America. He even shared how it was just him, his brother and his dad as he lost his mother in a car accident. We have always just accepted this part of Flynn and have never made him feel strange about it. Some of the things he knows about and the way he talks baffle us. He knows such incredible things about science, nature, animals, space and planets that he hasn't learned yet at school or at home. He is the most intelligent child and way beyond his years with his knowledge for a six-year-old. Even his teachers are mesmerised by his wisdom, and he also shares stories about his life in America. As they said to me the other day, it's as though he's just stepped off the plane from the US, even though he has never been there. I feel that being a conscious and awakened parent is such a gift to Flynn, as we now hold space for this part of him without judgment.

Seren also had a very interesting time when she was younger and would tell me she could hear and see other beings. At the time, I was a very different parent. I was living through fear, and my ego was running the show. I would tell her not to be silly or feel she was making it up. Imagine if we allowed ourselves to be part of the paradigm that accepted this and that living and existing in this way was the norm.

We are so blessed that our children go to an incredible school here in Australia where the norm is to climb trees, make fires, run around the earth barefoot, and hang out in the teepee. They each have an entire day where they spend it outside, amongst the trees in a place called the wild space. We have an incredible and wise Aboriginal elder who comes to the school often and talks to the children about walking with spirit. He teaches them about the spirit of the land and tells them they can always connect with spirit, and it's here to watch over them and keep them safe. He tells them how to connect with the land and the ancestors who have walked on this earth before them. I always get full-body goosebumps when I hear him talk to the children in this way. It's such a gift for them to connect outside of themselves and their bodies and to be connected more with the earth and a power far greater than us.

Moving Trauma from My Body

Through my spiritual healings, I was able to see that what happened to me as a child with a family member had a hidden gift within its centre. I was able to understand that someone can do something inexcusable to you, but you can learn to forgive them and continue through life. For the other person, I learned that he was able to do something inexcusable and be forgiven by another human. He died many years ago at a young age, and I always wondered what his next life would look like and whether he will carry some guilt and shame and not even understand where it has come from.

For me, my time at church taught me a lot. It taught me about forgiveness and letting the pain go, as, in the end it would only hurt me. However, over time, I began to feel that for me, I needed more than the word or forgiveness; I needed to shake and literally move the trauma from my body. I have been able to do that through meditation and breathwork. I believe that deep, conscious connected breath can remove lifetimes of trauma, and I have experienced this ten-fold in my own life. Many of the boundaries I set for my daughter came from fear—fear of her being hurt, lost, abducted or maybe even abused, but I knew I needed to learn to let this go—my life experiences were mine, and it wasn't right to pass these fears on to her.

When I was a young child, boundaries were never rational. Everything was in the heat of the moment and based on anger. The only real boundaries I knew were based on my ability not to cross my father's rules—those rules were pretty much I did as he said or else. If I ever spoke out of line or went against what he had said, then there would be a 'mighty one'. I can remember this as early as the age of three, but I am sure it happened well before that. I can still hear my dad saying, 'If you say no again, you will get a mighty one'. And of course, I would say no! I am still like that now, always strong-minded and going against the status quo. It's how I have been genetically made. The funny thing is, my dad is the same, so I wonder whether I triggered him and reminded him of a time when he was a child. Can you see the pattern forming here?

Taming the Beast

Unfortunately, all the 'mighty one's in the world would never tame the beast. Quite frankly, I am so glad the beast wasn't tamed! I certainly wouldn't be where I am now, and neither would my daughter. If we had just done as they said, gone along with the system, medicated Seren, drummed her down, and made her fit into society, then all the amazing healing, growing, and writing of books would never have happened. It's also important to say that parenting a strong-minded child is hard, and when they don't fit into the system, it's hard work. We have been very blessed to be able to send Seren to an alternative private school, as without this, I would have had to home school her. There is no way on this earth this kid could have fitted into the mainstream when she was younger, although this may change now that she is older and able to self-regulate more.

Recently, I hosted a live workshop in my private Facebook group, and I shared all about boundaries. There are different layers to it, but I want to give you examples from my life, so you will have that 'aha' moment and start to be able to witness why you have set boundaries in your life and how to see where they originate. When we have children, we don't consciously sit down and write down a list of boundaries for our newborn. We might have some ideas before the baby is born, and these are based on your values, upbringing, conditioning, and the country where you were raised. Different cultures and countries will evoke a need for different boundaries. Boundaries are simply put in place to keep your child safe. I feel that so many of us don't fully understand boundaries on a personal level, so it's even more difficult to put them into place for our children. One of my most respected and adored teachers comes in the format of someone I have never met personally, Dr. Nicole LePera, who wrote the Foreword for this book. I came across her on a social media app called Instagram. Nicole helped me to realise what I already knew but took me on a much deeper journey of inner wisdom and self-discovery. I truly believe we are born into the world with a knowing, but through conditioning, this knowledge is buried deep within. There are some ascended masters who have brought their wisdom and knowledge through and stood firm in their beliefs and compassion for others. When we break down their wisdom and knowledge, it is all the same voice. It's about love, forgiveness, and going within, it just often comes with a different flavour for each time in history.

Fear-Based Boundaries

Many boundaries are set within the moment based on triggers. We unconsciously set the boundaries that may have been placed on us a child. Then, we either tighten these boundaries, as our parents were so strict, or we loosen the boundaries, as our childhood had very little by way of boundaries. There are times when boundaries are essential—crossing the road, talking to strangers, not eating sweets for breakfast, lunch, and dinner, and keeping our bodies safe. These boundaries are essential, but I also feel so sad we have been conditioned not to talk to strangers. I must admit that is something I have never instilled into my children. We always talk to strangers! I have, though, taught them never to go off with strangers, even if they say Mummy and Daddy are ill. As Seren is now coming up to be a teenager and has a lot more freedom, we had some big conversations recently. Navigating a teenager with social media is hard, and we are continually talking about boundaries, just now in a different format.

Seren has a huge heart and recently on our road trip to Melbourne, we spent the afternoon seeing the sights and chatting to homeless people. Seren would always go over, introduce herself, ask them their name, and then sit with them. Se would tell them stories, talk to them about her dogs, their life, and ask them if they wanted food. We would then go off to purchase food and water for them. She would come back and give them food, some money and then carry on chatting with them. Men and women of all ages would smile and thank Seren. I would feel a connection between their hearts and hers, and it would often move Karl and me to tears.

Seren would tell me that some of our family would encourage Seren not to talk to the homeless people. They would tell her the homeless people would be taking drugs, and she shouldn't trust them. For me, it's bigger than that. Don't get me wrong; I used to feel like that, too, and we talk to Seren about that often.

> Trust everything my darling, even the painful and tough lessons. They can take us to the brightest of lights.

She tells me, 'Mum it's ok. I know intuitively which homeless people to approach. I can tell by their eyes'.

Trusting My Daughter

I am choosing to trust her, but again, we have educated her about drugs and how they can affect a person. We have also encouraged her to talk only to homeless people when an adult is present and always to stay safe. I feel this desire to help others is her golden light and her gift to the world. We have allowed ourselves as humans to walk past homeless people and not even look at them; it goes to show how disconnected we have become from love and humanity, Again, those were the teachings of Jesus that I was drawn to. He would go to the poor, the weak, and the sick and heal them, sit with them, and eat with them. He was love and embodied that, which is why I will never dampen Seren's sprit because of the old paradigm of fear and control.

Ask yourself the following questions. *What boundaries am I putting in place based on fear? Am I allowing what has happened to me to create strict boundaries for my child? Am I creating boundaries in my relationship based on things that have happened to me in my life? Is fear running the show?* Use your *Heal The Mother Journal* to work through this and journal. If you feel stuck, put on my Boundaries meditation, and then after the meditation, grab your journal and start to write. I often like to create an altar before I meditate. It's nothing fancy, but I grab the crystals I feel drawn to and place them next to me. I light some sage to clear the energy, I say a prayer, and then lay or sit to begin my meditation. You don't need to do that to meditate, but if you want to journal afterwards and you want to create that magical space and allow your higher self and your wisdom to flow through, this is a beautiful way to create it.

When I started to look at how I had set boundaries, they were always set in fear. The possibility that someone might take my child was a huge one for me. For years, I worried I would have a car crash, and I was so anxious pulling out onto main roads with the kids in the car. I am pretty sure I avoided big, public events for the last few years in the fear that I might lose a child. As any mother knows, the fear of losing a child makes you set some pretty big boundaries. In other ways, I am very laid back. Swimming has never bothered me. We have been the type of parents that even from a very young age allowed our kids to swim without armbands. We both had this inner knowing that while this can save a child, it can also stop them from learning to swim. Both Karl and I never really sat down and talked about this; it just evolved that way. All the children have been able to swim without armbands or support from around the age of three, and I am pretty sure Seren was around the age of two. They learned to swim underwater first and then started to get to swim above the water. All three of them learned to bob up to the top to breathe like a seal and then pop underneath again. It was miraculous as we never taught them to do that, but without the armbands, they naturally learned to do this.

I have seen other parents scream at the children when they even step near the ocean or a river, running down as if there was a shark. However, they are the parents that happily attend all the big events with the kids on their shoulders, waving a flag watching the fireworks, which would be my nightmare. I guess we all have our fears and our boundaries. For me, checking in with myself and seeing whether mine are fear-based and from my childhood, has helped me greatly.

I discovered that when we work through our boundaries, it gives our children a chance to be who they need to be in this life. What an honour that we get to work through our shadows and hold space for our children's light without dimming it for them. Of course, there need to be levels of boundaries; this is the role of a parent, and any animal in the wild would do the same thing, but for them, it is based on being in the moment, not pre-existing fears and anxieties. There are times in our children's lives when we need to do this, and I have all felt that in many instances. However, what I am saying is we should try and not place fears upon our child because something has happened to us.

Boundaries Born from Triggers

I want to explore trigger-based boundaries, as I call them because I feel so many boundaries are set this way, without us even consciously thinking about them. Most of life we are living in our subconscious, which means we aren't even consciously thinking about it. We are just living in the moment as our brain is already pre-programmed—mainly from our childhood—so depending on how that was for you, it will help you explore your boundaries and why you set them.

I feel deeply that the reason for my fear around losing the children is based on my traumatic childhood. There is so much I can't remember. I am pretty sure there is a reason for that, but while my conscious mind doesn't remember, my subconscious will be holding all the memories, pain, and trauma, which is how and why we can access those memories through hypnosis. I don't feel intuitively that I want to remember and relive those times, but wanting to keep my children safe stems from the very the fact that I wasn't kept safe. My dad was very strict in some ways, but also very loving in other ways. Despite the mighty ones, we were great friends and still are to this day. I always wonder where my mother was and why I don't have any memories of her. It's sad as I am sure there were some beautiful things she did, but my brain only remembers the bad.

To close on this subject, I want to share something with you that really hit home. A few years ago, my step-mum told me that my parenting was inconsistent. She said to me that most of the time, I was very laid back with the children, and she felt that I needed to be more disciplined, but when I was stressed or angry, I would tell the children off, and then they wouldn't understand as the parameters had changed. I never fully understood this concept, and to be honest, I was probably so deeply triggered by what she said, that I quickly moved on. When you have had a dysfunctional childhood, you want to do anything to make your children happy. But she was right; I was inconsistent, but I was so glad that she brought this up, even if at first, it triggered me.

That is how we can beautifully link triggers with boundaries. Triggers are our biggest teachers. We are being triggered every day, mainly by the people closest to us and most certainly our children. We often react with anger towards that person, or feel guilt, or shame. We feel it's their fault that they have made us feel this way. It is their fault they have pushed our buttons, but we don't sit with that and see it within us. There is much healing through our triggers. Before I began this work, when my children would trigger me, I would get angry, shout, or sometimes haphazardly put them on their room, which is something that I don't do anymore. I would have different rules based on my anger level, which I now see was based on the depth of my trigger. How far that wound went within me would be measured by the response. Some of my wounds spoke so loud to me, that it was clear to understand what they were:

- I am a bad mum
- I am not enough
- I am a failure
- I am not as good as the other mums
- I am failing my children

I wonder whether these were my own wounds, or maybe passed down to me from my mother. *Was I carrying her wounds into my own life without even realising it?* I had a deep-rooted belief that I would let my children down, the way my mum had let me down. Even saying that now, makes me feel so sad that I felt that way. I guess I always took the blame for my mum's behaviour, never blaming her and somehow feeling it was something I may have done. Maybe I wasn't a good enough daughter, or perhaps I could have done things differently, but I know that is not the case. She needed to do the work and make the changes, but sadly never did. But it's ok; it wasn't meant to be that way. It was always supposed to land with me to do the work.

We can all have some sort of negative belief about our parenting, even if we haven't had a bad childhood. When we have deep beliefs about ourselves and our parenting which simply aren't true, it can have a negative effect on our parenting. We hold this deep belief, it can be triggered, and then we set boundaries based on lack and fear.

I would often set boundaries in the heat of the moment based on what I perceived people around me felt. I would feel judged, I would feel my children would be judged, and then I would project that fear and lack onto them through tight boundary setting. Other times, I would feel so relaxed and happy that the boundaries would be loose, then they would cross the line or trigger me, and I would set strict boundaries. It was a never-ending nightmare and very stressful for both the kids and me. As I worked on my triggers and let go of the old stories about my mothering, I started to have a stronger sense of self, and our home became so much more harmonious.

Finding Tools to Support Myself

I had to dig deep to my core values, not my parents' values or the conditioning that had been so deeply rooted in my subconscious. Each trigger I would see as the guide. I would use meditation and journalling as tools to support my healing, and when I could, I would attend breathwork ceremonies to do deeper work. I would become clear on what felt good to me, and what my intuition was whispering to me. I started to rise as a mother and a woman. I have learned not to put boundaries in place based on fear and lack. I began to trust in my children and let them teach me. This work is teaching me how to 're-parent' them and myself! I allow them to run through puddles with bare feet, sleep in bed with me (even though they are six and eight), even Seren puts a mattress on the floor sometimes and sleeps at the bottom of the bed with our two doggies. Poor Karl sleeps in the guest room (but secretly loves it).

Before I was strict on these boundaries, but why? I guess because of conditioning, society, and values. I don't remember ever sleeping in my parents' bed—maybe only once and I was told to leave as I was wriggling too much. I don't want this for my children. I want them to have memories of feeling safe and loved, but you know what? I am not consciously thinking about it; I am letting them guide me. They want to sleep with me as they say it makes them feel happy and safe, and who doesn't want that? I was so focused on being a good mum that I read every book on sleep training when they were babies. I would feed, swaddle, rock, hush, and then lay them down to sleep. Every single one them was such easy babies that I honestly didn't get a lot of the issues that mums talk about. I put them through sleep training at such early ages—never cry it out, but very regimented and controlled. Why did I do that?

Probably the reason was that I wanted to be perceived as a good mum and be judged positively because I could do it. I had a deep feeling that people thought I would fail. I had been a bit of wild child since my teenage years, and although I was successful in many ways, I still had the part of me that was a bit cray-cray. Jokes about how I would forget the baby, drop the baby, or forget I even had a baby were constant. And the sad thing is, I would laugh with family and friends when they said those things, but I took my pregnancy, birth, and mothering so seriously. I had dreamt of it for so long and wished upon so many stars, and this new chapter was everything to me. It's funny that I was strict with my little newborn and toddler's sleep routine, yet here we are all in bed together, holding hands and drifting off to sleep at 8 pm! I shall remember these times with such fondness. However, it's also important for me to remember that if I suddenly change my mind and feel like my boundaries are being crossed and become triggered, then I could halt this sleep routine, and again the children could feel lost and confused. It's so important for me to change the boundary slowly and through love and tenderness. Luckily Karl loves sleeping alone, so, for now, this crazy, yet beautiful time is working for our family. After all, it's so important that you do you and do what works for your family. Listen to that beautiful intuition of yours!

Right now, these are my boundaries, and it been an incredible ride with the children, but Karl and I have talked about how when we get home from our road trip, they will be going in their rooms. Even thinking about this now makes me feel sad. I love listening to their stories before bed, the giggles, and the little things they loved about their day, this brings me true joy. I have decided that when we get back home, I will replace their bunk beds with double beds so I can still lie with them and chat. A couple of years ago when I was in the thick of my PMDD journey, which I now see was a massive awakening, I loathed these times. For one week of each month, I would find bedtime so hard that I would just want it over and done with as quickly as possible.

Too Scared to Sit with Myself

But you see, here is the thing. I was running from myself. I couldn't bear to sit in silence and lie with my children. My thoughts would race, I would start to feel overwhelmed, and I would begin to hate myself. It became so bad that for about two years, Karl would put the children to bed for that entire week. I would do everything—bath, clothes, prepare their little rooms—but then leave to clean up after dinner. It's an amazing contrast from where I am today, three years later. It's important to know that all this was happening at the time of my spiritual awakening. I felt like my world was imploding and crashing in on itself. The truth is that it was, but this is what happens. We are cracked wide open and may discover that everything we knew about ourselves simply wasn't true. We may find we have become an expression of our parents or society, and we have forgotten who we truly are. Undoing everything allowed me to begin the catalyst to my awakening and my metamorphosis. Whatever has happened to you or mistakes, you feel you may have made within your parenting, always trust that this is just a moment in time. Through your healing, you will have a chance to become the mother you were meant to be—trust, trust, trust.

Creating Healthy Boundaries

To finish this chapter, I want to share with you how to honour your boundaries. If you are already acing your boundaries, then good on you, girl, as this is a trait many of us don't seem to have. I swear this should be explained as part of our schooling. Never mind the Pythagorean theory; we need to know boundaries as children and young adults. If you are someone who had a challenging childhood, and you always felt you needed to strive for your parent's approval, you may struggle with setting healthy boundaries. If you are someone who didn't feel they received unconditional love from your parents, or maybe they had no boundaries, then again, you can suffer from an inability to set boundaries as an adult.

When we have come from families who either don't have boundaries or don't know how to allow us to honour our boundaries, again we can struggle. Then you can find yourself struggling to have healthy boundaries with your children. This has been my struggle. I have either had no boundaries, and everyone is free and easy. I start to feel like the best hippy-type mum in the world and like I'm a hairbreadth's away from dreadlocks, but then I get triggered, and I turn into a Victorian mother. Words shoot out of my mouth like:

'How dare you to talk to me like that.'

'I am so ashamed of you.'

They can shoot out like verbal diarrhoea, but then I check myself, calm down, and the hippie-wannabee mum with her tail in between her legs apologises profusely to her children. I have done this so many times, but at the end of the day, we are all trying to figure it out through love, so don't harbour any guilt towards yourself.

Over the last couple of years, I have worked consistently on my boundaries with myself, friends, and family. Instead of saying yes to things to make others happy or approve of me, I give myself time before replying, or I say I will think about it and let them know. The thought of doing such a thing before would make me feel horrible inside. I would worry people would stop liking me, or they would judge me. It was ridiculous, so I would say yes, then feel overwhelmed that I said yes, then cancel and hate myself for upsetting that friend or family member. I was simply unable to say no, even when I didn't want to do something and my intuition was screaming, *You don't want to do this.* I would feel a sense of shame for not doing something another person wanted me to do. Sometimes I would make poor judgments and perhaps say no when I needed to say yes. I just didn't know where the boundary was and was entirely lost within it all. I'd stopped listening to my intuition and was only guided by my ego while at the same time trying to be a constant people pleaser.

When I was in my early twenties, I had some of my clothes and cosmetics in a suitcase in the boot of my car. I would always go to friends' and family's houses and stay over. My mind would wander and be whizzing around. *Have I stayed with that friend or family member? Have I phoned that person or this person?* It was the most bizarre behaviour, staying everywhere like the littlest hobo and constantly wanting to make others happy. I had an awesome job in marketing for an international American bank. I spent my entire twenties working hard, partying hard, and constantly staying with everyone. I had no time to stop, I never let myself breathe for a moment, and I was on the go all the time. No wonder I crashed in my late twenties. I was exhausted!

I am finally at the stage where I can create healthy boundaries. I can do this with my time, my friends, children, family, and Karl. I can say no when others want me to say yes, and even though I can sometimes feel their angst at me, I feel solid in my body that I am honouring myself. I want to teach this to my children, and I can see which children need it the most. Seren is very headstrong and has no problem setting boundaries. She struggles with a certain friend, and I am trying to help her with that. It's funny that I am teaching this to Seren, but at the same time, she can trigger me for being so headstrong. However, she doesn't really need teaching. She is the one who has taught me! If she doesn't want to do something, she will happily say no with such a strong conviction, and she doesn't give monkeys who she upsets; what a trait, when we think about it. It's hard as a parent, but it's getting easier as she grows up.

Holding Space for My Spirited Child

From a very young age, Seren hated the beach and still does. In the summer, we like to spend as much time as possible at the beach. Seren would always stay at home. Every restaurant or cafe we go to, she hates, which was hard as she would often stay in the car. We realised we had to live our lives too, so sadly, we would go everywhere without Seren. She is the same person still, but she stays home or goes out with friends. A lot of people see it as defiance, but I am learning she's simply excellent at setting boundaries. She has some incredible traits that will serve her very well as an adult—determination, strength, resilience, a strong sense of self, great at boundary setting. That kid is going far!

Flynn is a dude, like Karl, very self-assured and has no problem at all setting boundaries, whereas Daisy is a people-pleaser. She won't even win a board game as she doesn't want to upset people. Karl and I are lovingly guiding her now, but at the same time, helping her to tap into her intuition. I feel if we honour our hearts and set boundaries from love and what our soul yearns for, we are honouring our soul's purpose.

It took me all my thirties to figure this out, and I want to teach this gift to you, so you don't have to take as long as I did to get there. One of the most amazing things someone taught me is replacing the word 'should' with the word 'could'. When you swap the word, it takes away so much of the guilt and shame we can place upon ourselves when we set our boundaries. Say it out loud to yourself about a situation you struggle with and see how much less guilt you feel. It's liberating, sister, let me tell you! The other thing that helped me so much is this: *What others think of me is none of my business.*

You need to read this over a few times, let it simmer, and let it land, as this is an important one! I had terrible boundaries because I was constantly worrying about what others would say about me. What would they say about marriage, my parenting, my weight, my skin, my hair, even my wrinkles? Karl would tell me, 'No one cares. They are too busy worrying about their stuff to worry about yours'. But those thoughts seemed to plague me. I have been called selfish so many times over the years by family, and even though I would still do my own thing, despite others trying to stop me, I would allow their words and feelings to be felt deep in my heart. I would do the things I wanted, but it would sit heavy on my conscience, which is never a good thing, as then you aren't consciously setting your boundaries. You are setting them but not really embodying them, and you are still allowing others to upset you.

Honouring Your Boundaries

When you first start to set your boundaries, you will notice that friends, family, or work colleagues may get upset with you. They won't recognise the new you, and the new healthy boundary version of you can trigger others. You may also struggle at first when you start setting your boundaries, but I would urge you to continue with the work. The more you do it, the easier it will become. I want you to journal in your *Heal The Mother Journal* some ways you would set boundaries for yourself. Maybe you need to explain to your boss that you are unable to take that extra shift or the additional project as you need to be at home with your family. Maybe you need to tell your mum that you will not listen to her berate your dad and their relationship anymore or vice versa. It could be explaining to your partner that you are taking some time for yourself as you need to fill up your mama cup. Whatever it is, write it down, and then start to free flow with your writing some ideas that can help you to put these boundaries in place. Use the boundaries guided meditation to help you do this, or even the chord cutting meditation can be so good for this exercise. If guilt comes up for you when you journal your boundaries, then cord-cutting will support you. You can begin to cut cords with the people or situations that make you feel guilty. It doesn't mean that you cut cords with them in real life; it means you let go of the energy attached between the two of you, and then setting boundaries will become easier. Remember, we are more than our bodies. We have an energy that can often be intertwined with others. Even past relationships can still have an energetic contract, and that can be freed by practising the Chord Cutting meditation.

Once you start to put boundaries in with the people around you, you will discover you can create healthy boundaries with your children. You don't feel that guilt for needing time for yourself, or feeling you are a terrible mum, which is the story I was telling myself for so long. I couldn't bear to think my kids didn't like me. I am now able to set boundaries calmly and without emotion and stick to them. I don't fly off the handle anymore when my children want more time on the iPad (when it's not an iPad day) or if they're going to watch a movie when it's a bath, book, and bed evening. I stay calm, I don't get triggered, and I remain firm in my boundary. It's funny how they see this now, and after getting upset and shouting and me, they suddenly stop and accept it. Before my boundaries were everywhere because I allowed myself to be triggered by the idea that I wasn't a good mum. This now doesn't happen and honestly is huge for me.

My mother spent the whole time being so upset with people and used to say, 'My whole life, I have done everything for everyone, and look where I am now'. In the end, she cut so many people out of her life—friends, family, even me and the children. She had turned to bitterness, which is so sad. You may find that certain people will struggle at first. Remember, you will be their trigger. You are holding up the mirror and reflecting all the parts from their lives when they weren't seen or heard. But it is not your job to do the work for them. Stay grounded in your truth, and step bravely forward as you do this work. You will start to find over time that your life will become like a poetic dance of the soul. You will begin to live your life based on your truth and your values. You stop becoming a people pleaser, and you free yourself. No longer are you a slave to others. You become a master of yourself.

CHAPTER 6
HEALING YOUR INNER CHILD.

So many experts are focused on fixing the child, when, in fact, the child who needs fixing the most is your inner child. The one who didn't feel safe heard, seen, or validated at times. The child who knew how to bring such joy into your life, but the one you have forgotten to connect with. It is time to reach out to your inner child, take her hand and walk the path together safely.

In this chapter, I will be teaching you how to connect with your inner child. We will learn how to work on loving her, listening to her, and allowing her to be present with you once again. We will also look at re-parenting yourself if you were someone who didn't have the loving security from your parents. This chapter is deep and can be revisited many times if you need.

This chapter is so close to my heart, as my childhood wasn't the best. I am sure my parents tried their very best, and I only hold forgiveness and love in my heart for them both, but I feel that is because I have done so much work on my inner child. As we explore this chapter together, I want you to know that it is possible to heal aspects of your inner child when you lovingly trust yourself to go to those spaces that we run from. So, let us begin some of the biggest work you will do in this book.

Walking with My Inner Child

Healing my inner child has been some of my greatest work and has helped me with everything from my relationships to my mothering journey, to learning to love and accept myself, and it even helped heal my PMDD. I love to share my journey with you, and I wanted to share that I have just had the most manageable period ever! If you remember what I shared with you about my PMDD and how I struggled for most of my entire life, for my period to just arrive every month, I am blown away! I did a gut, liver, and heavy metal cleanse some months ago, then I did my breathwork training, and since then my periods have arrived pretty much with ease each month. For anyone struggling with your periods, you can imagine that could be almost impossible, but I have achieved it, and it is why I want to help women heal. If I can heal something so big, we truly can heal anything—I honestly believe this. Breathwork and meditation allowed me to heal my inner child, and for the first time in my life, I was able to love myself fully.

I want to explain to you more about the inner child and firstly what this concept is all about. The inner child is based on our pre-programming, which is based on our subconscious. I have shared this before in other chapters, but I really want this to land for you. It's important that you understand how much of our childhoods play out in our adult lives, and how this can affect us years later. I will share my journey, but also Karl's, as it will give you an entirely different perspective.

Your Childhood Imprinting

First, let us look at Karl's childhood. Karl's mum is a soft, gentle, and caring woman. I have seen her give such tenderness with our children, and even with other children. She has worked with children for over 40 years and still gets so much joy from her job. I struggled with her outlook on Seren when she was first diagnosed with ADHD. She didn't fully believe in labels and felt the best we could do was to give Seren more love. We had quite a bit of upheaval in Seren's early years. We lived in five houses, once living in Australia for three months, and we also emigrated months after her sixth birthday. She also went to five different schools by the age of six. Karl's mum always felt Seren had gone through a lot, and that affected her behaviour. At the time, we didn't agree, but now I look back and see that she was so right! And Seren did need more love—buckets of it—so she was also right about that!

Karl had a beautiful childhood before his father left when he was eleven years old. He told me how his mum only gave him love as a child and as a growing teenager and adult. He never remembers her getting cross with him or shouting and losing it; she only gave him abundant love. She had the support of her parents, as Karl's dad worked away a lot, but Karl only remembers kindness and love. I have always been in awe at Karl's stress levels. He is so calm, even in a crisis, even in work, and with the kids. He always seems to be in rest and digest mode, and rarely in fight or flight mode.

The more I understand about childhood, the more I see how his mother has impacted who he is in this life. He has no fear of anything. It's like his imprinting is the calmest bluest ocean I have seen; it's such a gift. I feel this energy is deeply infused into both Flynn and Daisy. They are both so grounded and calm. I did so much work before I had Daisy and Flynn. I had peaceful, natural pregnancies and births. I feel their souls were able to enter this world and float here without picking up any of my baggage along the way. My darling Seren sadly picked up a lot from me—a toxic overload, unhealed pain and emotions, and childhood trauma. That kid got it all, although I am confident her spirit baby knew what she was coming into, and she chose our family for a reason.

Connecting with Our Spirit Babies

I am currently reading a book called *Spirit Babies* by Walter Makichen, and it shares how our spirit babies only come to us when they know we are ready. The book shares how parents and children have often been in each other's previous lives together. I have been told on numerous occasions that in a previous life, I was Seren's child, and she was my mother. We laughed at how true that seems, and we spend so much time, saying *'Seren you aren't the mum, honey'*. I still believe wholeheartedly that our children choose us, and I want you to know if you have a spirited child, just know that they chose you for a reason. You have a karmic contract in this life together, and all will start to make sense when you begin to heal. It's like the veil is lifted, and you can start to see who your child is and why they are here.

I only discovered recently that these children are known as angelic spirit babies, and they have possibly lived many lifetimes before. They have come to this life at this time because they see that they are here to help others; maybe that is why Seren wants to help homeless people. They have gone through their materialistic and egoic desires. They now only want to heal and raise the vibration of this planet. They can also be known as indigo children. Let your mind wander back to you as a child. Think back to your childhood. *What were your parents like with you? How was your home? Did you feel loved, safe, seen, and heard? Did you have an imaginary friend? Where you also spirited? What did you want to be when you were older? What were your dreams?* Think back to that child, let your mind wander and re-connect with your inner child; she may help you at times to know who your child is.

We must try to not hold any resentment towards our parents, and allow those feelings to come up and journal them while holding in your heart that there is a reason you chose your parents—and always send love and compassion. When we go through this work, it can bring up anger, but again, trust everything and know this work is about healing and letting go and not giving space for blame or guilt. You can use your *Heal The Mother Journal* to start free-flow writing. If you need help with this, I would suggest listening to Dr. Nicole LePera's Healing Your Inner Child meditation and then journalling afterwards. A lot can come through us when we are in such a relaxed state. When we meditate, that is the place that is able to access our higher self and higher consciousness, the part of you that allows for truth, love and compassion. Trust yourself and let yourself go there.

Carrying Your Parents' Fears

I have shared with you about my childhood, but what's also important to note is my mother suffered from various phobias. She had a stomach ulcer and was convinced she was going to get another one. She would tell me that if she had aspirin, she would die. She was also confident that she had throat or tongue cancer and would say to me that she thought she had cancer, even though she didn't. She was also scared of lifts, driving on freeways, driving in cities—basically anywhere unless it was near our small village home. She was afraid of flying, and I am sure for that reason we didn't go on holiday abroad until I was around twelve, as my mum wanted to escape my dad. It was a holiday, but she also said it was 'to get away from the bastard'(nice). Shortly afterwards, when I was thirteen or fourteen, she took me to Greece again 'to get away from my dad'. She allowed me to get drunk with her and some English and Greek men that we met. She then left on a motorbike with one of the Greek guys and left me with the English men. I am hoping that she was a good judge of character, but I guess honestly, I was just fortunate. I left the night unscathed other than a chipped front tooth from a Budweiser bottle, but seriously, it could have been so much worse. I got a lift home on the back of a motorbike, thanked the English guy, and went home to find my mother passed out. I probably had the time of my life, but looking back, it's only one of the examples where my mother had no boundaries. As I have shared before, it is also probably why I have struggled so much with creating healthy boundaries for my children in the past. My rules and limitations were based on fear and worry that I could lose my child. I don't feel that way anymore. So much of my anxiety and fear as a mother has now gone, and I can be fully present as a mum and enjoy my children.

Also, what's important to see here is that my mother raised me with a lot of personal fears. She was anxious about everything, she cried a lot, she smoked and drank a lot, and I only feel sadness for her. I think she was so haunted and needed to do some deep inner work, but back then, we didn't have the healing tools we have right now. We are genuinely in one of the most awakened times in history. It's an absolute blessing to be on the earth right now and to have this knowledge and healing potential at our mercy. That is why I hold no judgment towards my mother. She made those choices and thank God I have always been ok. I genuinely believe I had a guardian angel looking after me, as I have been in some pretty vulnerable situations over the years, but I have always been safe. For that, I am eternally grateful.

Sometimes I wonder whether I now feel like this because I have done so much work on my inner child. There is so much I have been able to work through and heal. I have made peace with my childhood and learned to let go of so much I was holding onto. I came to learn that a lot of fears I have had in my life were not my own but passed down to me from my mother by imprinting. When I look back and remember the driving phobia I shared with you, I can now see it wasn't my fear, but it was simply passed down to me from my mother. The London bombs incident that happened to me shifted everything and allowed childhood trauma and suppressed pain to rise to the surface. I feel it was always there lying dormant, and then it needed something to unearth it. Like an earthquake discovering a hidden secret, it needed something dramatic to allow it to rise and be seen.

In healing this part of myself, I have discovered so much about me that I wouldn't have ever found if I hadn't been triggered by a traumatic event. It was that catalyst I feel was in my life for a reason—to bring to the surface all that needed to emerge. As the Chinese philosopher Lao Tzu said, '*When the student is ready, the teacher will emerge.*'

This saying means so much to me, as it is what I believe is happening to so many of us as we heal. For me, healing is becoming conscious to thy self and therefore becoming present to who we are in this life. To begin the path to healing means we are brave enough to remove the mask and look past the veil of control, pain, and fear. Once we begin this work, we can find that rarely will the mask go back on, but when it does, it will feel so uncomfortable we will feel it in our very core. For me, that realisation is anxiety—I look at this only as a guide, here to wake us up to the fact that we are entirely out of alignment with who we are. We have come off course, and the anxiety we feel is simply a way of waking us up to this. I never look at my anxiety as a bad thing, but merely go within during meditation and allow it to tell me why I feel anxious. Our higher self knows the answers to our anxieties.

Feeling Unworthy

As my work is changing and I am about to publish this book, feelings of unworthiness and anxious thoughts have been popping up again. I understand that it's my ego trying to keep me safe as I am expanding, stepping into my authentic self, and rising, but all that positivity can be met with resistance. Many people get to this point and then stop. They allow their conditioning, early childhood programming, and fears to stop them truly rising. Be mindful when you feel this in your body. Ask yourself, *Where do I feel this discomfort?* It could also be a physical pain, as well as something psychological or emotional.

Years ago, whenever something big would happen in my life, my back would go into spasm. I would be in agony and unable to walk or drive, and it would last for weeks. I saw experts and spine specialists for twelve months, and they were even talking of operating on my back. I discovered that it was in fact my emotions causing the pain after I read a book called *Healing Back Pain: The Mind Body Connection* by John E. Sarno, MD. My emotions had become so sneaky and would manifest as debilitating back pain. When I realised this, it didn't hold a strong grip on me anymore, and I was able to shift this pain through essential oils, EFT (tapping) or meditation. Trust these nudges, feel into them, and use your future-self journalling to guide you back love and go forth into your expansion. Fear not—remember you are in the driving seat, and fear is merely a passenger beside you!

We can also access our inner child through mirroring. How our children act towards us and in their life can often be them reflecting our pain. What we feel, they will feel, and they will act it out until we have healed. I spend a lot of time talking about the healing of a woman as I truly believe that once we heal, our children heal, and this can ripple out to our partners, family, and even friends.

A couple of years after my awakening, Karl went through his, but I don't believe that would have ever happened if I hadn't manifested, encouraged, and paved the way for him to crack wide open. I was able to guide and support him through his process, and it's been such a beautiful and deep connection for us both. Many people would ask me how I managed Karl to awaken and my answer is twofold. We must go first and take the brave steps of healing. Once your partner sees the changes in you, they may also decide that they want this too. Manifesting is a powerful tool—write down what you want in your *Heal The Mother Journal*. Write an open letter to God or the universe stating what you want, pray on this word, meditate on it and start to visualize your partner going through this process too. It took Karl a few years, it wasn't instant, but when it happened, it surely was worth the wait.

Helping Your Partner to Awaken

I would encourage you to chat with your partner about your healing journey. Often women will tell me, *I am healing, I am doing the work, but my partner is not.* Having them do this work with you can be incredible, but trust your instincts, you will know what to do. If it feels like you can talk to your partner, then start to talk. Maybe they need you to do the work first; perhaps they want to do this work with you. They can also use guided meditations. I believe we are part of a massive awakening. The feminine energy is strong on our planet now, the goddess energy is once again coming forth, and it's an exciting time for a change. If your partner is not ready, do not worry. Do the work anyway, trust in the process, and have faith their time will come.

When you heal and awaken, you allow the portal of light to pass through you. It will shine out to the world, and your environment will change. You will begin to see a shift in others around, your friendships may change, and the circles that you move in may change. Some of my friends in the UK now live a very

> Our child's anger and anxiety can reflect our shadows.

different life to me, but the thing is they haven't changed, I have. They are still having so much fun, partying at the weekend, being wild and whilst I love them deeply, they are like my sisters, I could never go back to that way of living. For me now, a full moon women's circle, a breathwork ceremony, a spiritual festival in the hills or drumming with others on the beach under the full moon—for me this pure joy. I can never go back to the person who I once was but have endless thanks and love for that part of myself. It is so powerful when you finally answer the call to your healing—you finally come home to yourself.

Holding Up the Mirror

The child is mostly connected to the mother, so whatever you have going on within you, can be mirrored out through the child. I always thought it would come through in my oldest child's behaviour, but very recently, I was able to see that all our children have messages of healing and growth for us. Often their behaviour will only change when we heal that part of ourselves.

If you have a child struggling with anxiety, allow that mirror to be reflected to you, and ask yourself, *Do I have to suffer from anxiety and worry? Does their father, or another family member that is close to your child suffer from anxiety and worry?* Allow that mirror to be reflected, and you will be given your answers. *Does your child have issues with anger?* Again, allow the mirror to show your answer lovingly. You will often be spellbound by what you see. Be honest with yourself, step aside from your ego, and allow your heart and intuition to guide you, not your head.

My daughter Daisy was the catalyst to awakening some of my deepest, darkest childhood pain. I always thought it was Seren who would heal me; after all, she was my challenging, spirited child. She has taught me so many lessons, but the lesson of anger would come from my beautiful, peaceful Daisy Belle. She has always been such a peaceful and easy child since her incredible birth. She was born at home in a birthing pool, and her birth has been watched on YouTube 360,000 times. I used to be a HypnoBirthing practitioner and wanted to teach the world that labour didn't need to be painful and something to fear; I wanted to show it could be something of power and magnitude.

Daisy was born en-caul, which means she was born in her amniotic sac. The second midwife told me the birthmarks on Daisy, one each on her leg and lower back, meant that she was very spiritual. I now see the lessons Daisy needed to teach me. It needed to be her; she was my peaceful, calm, and ever-present child, so when her anger started at around seven, she was the person who could wake me up to my healing. I wouldn't have noticed it with Seren. I would have put it down to her impulsivity and her ADHD. Yet, when Daisy started this behaviour, I knew I had to go deep.

Daisy's anger has been wild of late! Kicking, biting, scratching, yelling, and throwing things; it's been a force to reckon with and hard to watch as my peaceful daughter turned into the Tasmanian devil. Last night, it reached a peak. I handled it poorly, yet even here is a lesson. She hit me, and I hit her back. She screamed at me, and I yelled back at her. I put her in her room and told her she wasn't to come out to be with the family until she had calmed down. That is precisely what happened to me, but much worse. I would be smacked and shamed by my dad, but when I look back, I did the same to Daisy. This is not something I do with the children, but I am sharing this as I know there will be so many mamas who need to hear this. We are only human, and we make mistakes, but seeing the reason we made that mistake, why we were triggered and acted that way is healing. Being brave enough to turn the light on our shadows is how we transcend as better humans and parents.

The Old Parenting Paradigm

For a long time, I would joke about my dad's behaviour. We would laugh as a family, and make jokes about it, but writing this book allowed me to see that maybe he made those choices because of his childhood. My dad still says he had a great childhood, and he doesn't need to go back there. I am not saying it was wrong because that is how it was in those days. But the follow on from that is we are raising wounded children and carrying on the pain and fears from generation to generation. *This generation is the one where it stops.*

My dad's whole parenting paradigm was about control and fear. Chatting to my dad, that is the way my Grandma raised him. He told me my grandad worked hard, and he rarely saw him during the week, but it was my Grandma who was strict at home. I loved my Grandma dearly, but she had very little time for tears or sadness. 'Get on with it' is how she raised my dad. She was very stoic and had no time for tantrums or tears. I remember once when Seren was two and wanted my attention. 'Ignore her', she would say. That was just my Grandma, and she had been amazing to me when I was a child but had no time for 'child's play'. Make-believe play was discouraged when I was a child. We did spend hours laughing, baking, sewing, and singing 'Somewhere Over the Rainbow' together, which I loved so much. But, when I think back, what we shared were the things Grandma loved. I don't remember her ever being cross with me, but I found it so surprising when she would tell me to ignore Seren. I wanted to cuddle her and love her if she was having a tantrum and be there for her, but Grandma's way was to ignore. I wonder where that goes back to? Perhaps not being seen or heard as a child? My dad's words that he used all the time were 'children should be seen and not heard'. So many times, as a parent, I have heard myself sound like my parents, but for the last twelve months, I have worked very hard not to use such words as shame or make my children feel guilty for their behaviour.

Connecting with My Inner Child

Last night as I sent Daisy to her room, what I really did was send my inner child and pain away. It's too hard to face it, sit with it, and go deep into it, so instead, I shut it out. I will close the door on it, tell it that it's naughty, badly behaved, and cannot be with us. That is what I did with Daisy, but if we reflect the mirror upon ourselves, we can see the child is simply the messenger of our inner child. Our children are our greatest teachers. I have known that for a long time, but it's only been the last few days through Daisy that I have seen how prevalent and true this is in our lives.

I shared my experience yesterday in my private Facebook group, and so many of the mothers shared the same feelings. They shared issues with their mothers that they hadn't dealt with, how they were struggling to step into this new type of parenting. As we shift the consciousness of others, including teachers, it can be challenging, but I feel the more we do the work, the more we can inspire and empower others. I remember doing it with one of Seren's teachers. I shared how Seren triggered me, and I used control to parent her, but then I shifted my parenting. I told her I didn't see Seren as defiant anymore, but a child who needed deep love and reassurance. This amazing teacher changed her teaching with Seren overnight and went from a Draconian style to the most loving and compassionate teacher. Seren even now has such a deep love for this teacher, and at one point said her teacher was her best friend. *That is the power love and kindness have.* We can heal, and then we share this and help others to rise and break free of the conditioning and control. Remember, most of us have been raised like this, so we are walking around with pain bodies reacting to every single situation in life like that wounded child who hasn't healed yet.

What I realised over the last several days is that the buck stops with me. I always knew that I was partial to the odd door slam, losing it some mornings and shouting at everyone when they weren't ready for school. I would yell at Karl in a premenstrual way, sometimes cry and be so far away from the Mary Poppins-style mother I thought I would be. I would tell myself not to be unkind, and that all mothers lose it at times. I honestly felt that these fleeting moments, albeit every moon time, wouldn't affect my children. Most of the time, I was a loving, caring, devoted mother, but I realised in Daisy that this behaviour had affected my children. It was now playing out in Daisy through her anger, the lashing out, and the anger she had been displaying. It showed me I had not dealt with some serious issues that happened to me as a child. My inner child was wounded, and as I hadn't dealt with her, acknowledged her, and loved her, *Daisy was my awakening to the need for this healing.*

The morning came, and even though Daisy and I had sat down last night and acknowledged her feelings, she still displayed anger and rage in the morning. I am trusting that everything happens in divine timing, and there will be many more lessons and healing for me to go through. The night before we sat on the sofa cuddling, and we talked about the colours that she saw when she was angry. It intuitively came to me. I honestly had no idea where I was going with it. I had probably read it somewhere, but it seemed like a great place to start. Daisy told me how she saw red when she was angry, but how it upset her so much when I would be angry back at her. She

How we raise our children is how they will raise their child. If we want to change the future, it must begin with us.

said that made the red turn to blue, which meant sadness and that to be happy she needed to get to green; a pretty good analogy for a seven-year-old! We talked about breath and how it was something Daisy could use to change the blue or red feelings to green. Daisy said that she would try it but again said, 'Mummy when you get angry back at me, it makes me sad'.

Entering the Fighting Arena

Why did I enter the fighting arena with my child when she gets angry? Why did I put on my armour and start a fight, even when I hadn't chosen to fight the battle? The one reason is my wounded inner child—a child who hasn't been seen, heard, accepted, or fully loved, a child who wasn't allowed to show anger, frustration, or speak their feelings, a child who was parented through control and fear. I am pretty sure my ego is at play, too, that part of ourselves that is always trying to protect us and look after us, that part of ourselves that won't allow for spiritual growth, the part of ourselves that told me for too long that my anger wouldn't affect my children. Now, here I can witness that it would affect them, and it would mainly affect my peaceful child, but we could both learn from this.

When Daisy's anger and anxiety peaked on this occasion, it also happened to be by 'moon time'. I shared in the previous chapter how this affected me so much, but I am now able to see the gift within, each trigger, each wound. I allow this time to let it be and go within to heal it. This moon time, Daisy started to have some issues which I feel were so much highlighted because of my moon time. Her anxiety about school had reached fever pitch, and for some reason, I wasn't coping with the behaviour. It manifested itself as anger and rage in Daisy, and I don't always respond well to that type of behaviour. Interesting that I have never really dealt with my anger, so I guess that is why I struggle so much. Karl, on the other hand, is so calm, and I very rarely see any type of anger in him. Therefore, it's not a trigger for him, and he's able to handle this sometimes so much better than me.

When Daisy responds in her way, I see her reflecting out to the world my inner shame and the guilt around my anger. It's been an issue of mine since I was a teenager, possibly even a child, but I can't remember that as much. The shadow I tried to conceal and hide from the world was now coming through my beautiful seven-year-old daughter, Daisy. We live in a society that wants to fix things right now! If your child's behaviour shows them to be hyper, anxious, or defiant, it may be suggested by the school that they see an expert. We want to make everything right, fix it, make it go away, but here's the thing that we are missing—through us, our child will reflect our shadows to the world. Our pain, anxiety, suffering, and trauma can be mirrored through them. When we allow ourselves to go inwards and work on our healing, we allow ourselves to heal. I have learned that in turn, we can heal our children. There are so many experts across the world trying to heal our children's behaviours. There are so many ideas, concepts, programs, and sadly, medications that are now in place, trying to help our children from as young as toddlers. I feel if we use the mirror, and instead of looking at our child, we go within and look towards our inner child—we will find the missing key.

Healing My Outer Circles

All my work has been self-taught and self-learned. I have read a few amazing books that have changed my life and my learning over the last couple of years. The more I would lean into this work and heal, the more my children would heal. The more my marriage would heal, the more my friendships and work would blossom. I started to realise this work was everything my soul knew to be true. I would be continuously guided to write and share this work, and the more I did, the more other people would thank me. They would share their awakening moments with me. They too would share that as they heal their child would heal too.

I started to see the importance of this work and understand that everything I was learning was real and true. The fantastic

Dr. Nicole LePera, connected with me a couple of months ago. I reached out to her and shared my passion for normalising ADHD, learning to manage it holistically, and my healing with both ADHD and PMDD. Nicole interviewed me for her YouTube channel, and it was there that she helped me to see what I was doing in my family and teaching others to do the same would change lives.

She confirmed to me as we chatted that our children are our mirrors. We talked about how when our child triggers us or others, it is simply a childhood trauma of the adult that they have not dealt with. Childhood is a time in our lives when we are learning so much about the world around us, yet we are often told to be quiet, calm down, not to shout out, and not to express our ideas. We're told to be small, not be seen or heard, and it is validated to us that we are not important or worthy. Those traits and feelings run deep into our subconscious. No wonder so many decisions are based around fear, lack, and scarcity; that is what has been portrayed to us since we were children. Nicole made me see that everything I was learning, or unlearning, was powerful, and having that support and validation was such a gift to me.

The day that Daisy's rage kicked in, straight away, I felt mine react. *Why did I do that? Why did I enter the craziness so quickly when the madness wasn't mine to enter? How many of us do this, though?* So many of us go into the point in time with our partners, children, family, or even strangers. We only must think of football matches or brawls in clubs or fights. It can start with just one person but can scale into a full-on brawl with sometimes hundreds of people. Now I see this tendency isn't only people here; it is years of childhood trauma and pain bodies that are so big and heavy, they are willing to get into fights with people they do not even know or with whom they haven't exchanged any words. During my moon time, I would enter this realm so easily. In the past, I have had arguments with completely random strangers. I would feel they were rude to me, and I would openly tell them, which would often get into some sort of angry exchange. I couldn't see at the time it wasn't truly me, but my shadows and pain body were simply mirroring out to the world.

We managed to get Daisy to school this day through tears and tantrums, and I was glad Karl stayed so calm and present. I really needed someone else to hold the space for me, as I was not holding it very well myself. That is one of the most beautiful sides of an awakened family. It has taken Karl two years to get this point of awakening, and as I write this now, he has just flown off the US to start a 10-day trip of a new awakening path for himself. I am so honoured to see him do this inner work!

Sitting with The Anger

When they left for school, I waved through exasperated tears and frustration and then closed the door. I kicked a toy and then even harder, kicked the kitchen stool. For the first time, I was able to witness this anger, this powerful emotion, and I remembered what I had learned in Bali in the breathwork course. *Sit with the uncomfortableness of your emotions and let them teach you.* We are never taught this about anger. We are made to feel guilty and shameful about anger. After all, it's the one emotion that can get us in so much trouble. It can hurt people, ruin lives and break up relationships, but is it really the anger or the hidden pain and suffering dying to come out and be set free?

I sat on the floor in the kitchen cross-legged and said out loud, '*What do you have to teach me'?* I closed my eyes and started to breathe. I started with some conscious connected breath—in through the nose and out through the mouth without pausing—and allowed my subconscious to take me where it needed. It was here that I saw two separate childhood traumas come to me in a flash. I was able to witness them and feel into the power and magnitude they still held on my heart and soul. Allowing myself to see these memories and feel their strength, helped me to feel how much anger and resentment I was still holding in my body. I used my journal and shined the light on the dark shadows that I had forgotten. Illuminating them, honouring them, and writing them down helped me to heal them and set them free.

Gone are the days when we feel we can't work on ourselves because we must do everything for our children, and let our needs go last. This is an old paradigm which I believe it was causing life-long generational disease and suffering. My mother had every type of phobia possible, plus an addiction to cigarettes and alcohol. In my younger years, I was the same. I was a smoker, and although I would never say I was an alcoholic, I had a problem with alcohol in my late twenties. I would drink until oblivion, and while apparently to my friends and partner, it was hilarious (I was always the happy, drunken clown), it was learned behaviour. I truly believe that so many fears I had I were inherited from my mother. Just like we inherit our skin, hair, and eye colour, so do we inherit such things as fears and phobias. I would encourage you to work on healing any shadows you have so they don't pass down onto your children.

> Once we shine the light on our shadows, we can finally turn them into light.

Peeling Back the Layers

Over the years, I have struggled with so many phobias, but I have been strong enough to learn how to manage them. Hypnosis, human givens, new age healing, RTT, EFT—I have tried them all. As I drove along the freeway yesterday, happily chatting with a friend after avoiding freeways for almost a decade, I realised the gift I was giving to my children. Last month, I flew to Bali by myself; six months before that, I took three flights to America. One of the biggest reasons I did that was to learn to be alone (this is huge for me), and to unlearn all the behaviours and patterns my mum had unconsciously imprinted into me, so I don't have to imprint these into my children.

A transitional character is a person who in a single generation, changes the entire course of a lineage, who somehow finds a way to metabolise the poison and refuses to pass it on to their children. They break the mould. Their contribution to humanity is to filter the destructiveness out of their lineage so that the generations downstream will have a supportive foundation upon which to build productive lives. Carlfred Broderick, PhD.

Remember what I said about choosing your parents? My spirit baby knew what she was getting into; she would have known that my mother struggled with her addiction and my father with his mental health, yet she still decided to come at this time. If my mother had done all the work, it would never have been passed down to me to do this work. I would never have learned all the beautiful lessons that I have. I would never have discovered my gift for writing, and you wouldn't have this book in your hands now.

Through my children, I was able to understand about triggers and boundaries that would eventually lead me down the path of connecting with my inner child. I learned that how I was treated in my childhood was now playing out in my children. I understood how much I could learn from my inner child. I was able to go back through meditation, breathwork, and journalling and connect with her once again. I was able to feel her pain as she was not allowed to be seen or heard. She witnessed more than a child should ever witness, and there were some awful things my mother said to me that were still etched on my heart.

Words Can Hurt

As I shared before, my mother would tell me that she loved me, but she didn't like me. She would say to me that she would forgive me, but she would never forget. Even though my grandparents were amazing with me, they would get upset sometimes if I would act like a child. Through a session of RTT, I was able to witness a time when I was pretending to be a puppy and barking on the floor in front of my grandparents.

'Stop being so babyish, Susy, and stop doing that', I was told.

I can't remember how old I was, but this memory had made me feel shameful, and it was deeply etched in my mind. Through RTT and working on the inner child, I was able to release the memory and see clearly that it was never about me; it was about them. It might seem like a silly thing, but for it to come up through hypnosis means that it was deep enough in my subconscious to come to the surface. I needed to honour it, shed light on it, take away the shame, and release it.

My father would take away my Gee-Gee, and that was a form of punishment along with a mighty one. Again, it was an act of shame towards me, but it was never my fault; working on my inner child has allowed me to see this finally. This chapter is a hard one for me to write, and I have been journalling and listening to the Inner Child meditation to support me with this work. It brought up a lot of feelings, and as I have gone back to edit it, it brought up even more emotions. A lot came up for me, which I haven't shared in this book, but there were some very traumatic events that I hadn't processed. It was only during this chapter that I began to heal them and let them go. Daisy is next to me while I am trying to edit, asking me to make cookies with her. I am trying to explain to her to ask Daddy, who is in the kitchen making pancakes, but she is so adamant. With Karl's support, I left the bedroom and headed upstairs to finish editing. I sat down and started to cry; this release was so important. Never be afraid of your tears, let them out, even cry up to the sky, hold up your chest, release it and let it go—this is your time. This work is profound and so needed, so please always give yourself the space to do it, even saying no to cookie baking—your healing is so important and needed for your family. The universe will test us with distractions but stand firm in your healing journey and remember you could be releasing generations of pain, so make it count!

Healing Can Be Confronting

Going back to these pain points and memories can be tough, so give yourself time for your space and healing. Use the guided meditations, get yourself into nature, shake your body, and have healing, as the inner child can be deep work. As I started to cry, I felt anger towards my mother. *Why did you have a child when you weren't able to parent me, love me and keep me safe?* I understand that is just the wounded ego, but by connecting with my heart, I am thankful that she gave me life. Even though it hurts, I have so much to be grateful for, and I love the life I have been able to create. If a lot is coming up for you, keep using your journal and your future-self journalling. It's important we create a new future, re-write the book and consciously change our pre-programming.

Understand that the generations before us may not or will not be able to do this work. Our parents or grandparents may not understand why we need to do this work. They may feel that other children had it much worse, but again, be aware of triggers. Stay in your light, keep doing the work, and eventually, they will see the incredible changes in you and your family.

I believe that once we do the work on our inner child, we should allow the journey to keep moving. I feel it's essential we don't get stuck here. We do the work, connect with our inner child, honour the feelings, and then let go. I feel I was stuck in my painful childhood for so long. These issues were playing out in my teens, my twenties, and even my thirties, as I didn't start working on my inner child properly until I was forty years old. For so long, I would talk about my childhood with different boyfriends, who were in their twenties, and of course, didn't want to hear it. Then with Karl, it would play out again and again, but he felt, you should just get on it with it and not go back over your childhood. I wanted to, I really did, but I knew how much it was affecting my life. I am so grateful to have had the tools to help me move this pain and trauma through my body. I feel so honoured to have been able to do this work, and my dream is that by sharing my story and giving you these tools, all of which you will find in Chapter 10, you too can honour this part of yourself.

Moon Time Madness

As I edit this chapter, it's highlighting my issues around my moon time and anger, yet I still feel there is work to be done. Yesterday I listened to the Inner Child meditation. I closed my eyes and allowed myself to journey through a different child-hood home. It was interesting as I saw myself in the house I lived in during my teens. I was able to see my mother with all her fury, rage, and anger, crying, and smashing plates. I could feel all the feelings, sadness, and bewilderment that I would have felt at age twelve. I was able to see how this has had such an impact on my adult life, and while I have broken many generational curses, this one can still plague me at times. The saying, 'monkey see, monkey do' came to mind, and I realised there is still work to be done. I do not want my children to see this and repeat it with their children; I must break this pattern.

I found a book which I will share with you in Chapter 10, as I will put all the resources in here for you. I started to listen to this audiobook, and as I began to listen to the words about anger, I saw how much it resonated with me. It talked so much about how women often get angry as they don't feel seen or heard. That is precisely what happens to me. Karl can't deal with any type of anger, so as soon as I show a slight resemblance to anger, he starts to make remarks about my childhood—I am damaging the children, etc., which ironically makes me angrier. We have an awesome relationship, but this has always been the dark shadow in our relationship. As soon as I listened to chapters of this book, I saw that this was going to be the book that would help me. It's like it's been written for me! It's for women and teaches you how to turn your nagging, moaning, and blaming anger into a positive channel to turn around aspects of your relationship! It also highlights the issues with the other person. It teaches us that our anger will never be able to change them but how we can channel this anger without the emotion to bring harmony to our relationships. It also teaches you how to manage your relationship and your anger and upset with your parent. It talks about boundaries and how to put these in place with a parent when they criticise your parenting or you. It really has been such a fantastic tool to help me move through this final part of my healing.

So, for me, revisiting this work through writing this book has made see there is still much work to be done. I am not an angry person at all outside of my relationship, and watching Daisy makes me realise she is the same. In a family of five and being the middle child and the smallest, she uses her voice to be seen and heard. I now see that by changing my anger and using it for good for our relationship, I can help Daisy to do the same in our family. Like me, she never displays anger outside of the home. I understand her completely. She is the mirror, and I feel honoured that she has reflected the part of me that needs healing. How wonderful it would be for me to change that part of myself and then to help Daisy. That is why this book is so essential; *Heal The Mother, Heal The Child* is such deep, potent and beautiful work. It is not easy, and I commend you so much for doing this work and learning to reparent yourself. Never underestimate how amazing you are, and what a gift you are to your future lineage. Always hold this in your heart, especially during the hard days.

> **The answers we seek to heal our children are often hidden in the shadows of a mother's pain, guilt, fear, and shame. We cannot hold space for our children's needs until we have first healed our aching souls.**

Do Not Underestimate the Power of Prayer

Never feel shameful about your behaviour. See the gift within and understand there is a reason as to why you are displaying the behaviour. Through shining the light on it and asking for help from the universe, we can start to reparent ourselves the way we would have liked or hoped to be parented. Yesterday I said a prayer, and then moments later, I found myself meditating.

Then I discovered the anger book. Prayer isn't a religious thing, for me, but I truly believe we have guides helping us through life. Asking aloud I find is more powerful and quicker than asking in our heads. Let your prayers be heard and send them up to the universe! You can simply ask the universe, God, source, or your guides—do whatever resonates with you.

This is a prayer I like to use: *Universe/God, please help me, please guide me, and please teach me. Please show me the tools I need to work on my healing.*

Sometimes I will get down on my knees and pray. Or I will have a good cry in the shower and pray there. I find the shower one of the most cleansing tools. Sometimes it's like a portal. I have the most amazing ideas and breakthroughs in the shower. I feel like in some ways I am releasing and letting go. Do whatever works for you. So much has happened for me when I have asked God or the universe for help. Let your voice be heard!

I only hope I have done enough work, so my children don't have to go through the same thing, but if they need to, I hope they will let me help and guide them through it. I am open to understanding what mistakes I made and taking it all on board. I do believe my parents tried their best. Although I do not have a relationship with my birth mother, I still respect and honour her for bringing me into this world. I am learning that we had a karmic contract and while we didn't make in this life, maybe we will be together again in another lifetime. There is always work to be done in every lifetime—for us all. We are merely souls passing through different times and spaces, possibly even at the same time, which is an interesting concept also.

I want you to journal about some of the things that were said to you as a child. Write down the negative ones but also the positive ones and see how they have shaped the person you are today. My mother always told me that the world is my ocean. She would say to me that I was strong because she is strong. She was an avid writer and poet and genuinely wanted to help the world. She was on the TV and the radio, always trying to get her point across and do good in the world—these positive traits I have taken from her and have been able to use for the greater good. I am deeply grateful for those gifts, as they have served me well. I have put them to good use, and I am profoundly grateful. My father always told me 'debts and relationships'. He would say to me repeatedly that those were the things that I needed to work on. I have no debt, and my twenty-year relationship with Karl is stronger than ever, so for these words of guidance I am genuinely grateful. I feel that those things were their gifts to me, and I have so much thanks in my heart to both of them. I want you to see that even if you had a challenging childhood, there would always be light. Shining the light on the darkness is important, but always allow yourself to remember some of the beautiful moments in your childhood too.

Remember the Light as Well As The Dark

As we work through the inner child work, it's essential that we honour the darkness, but we also honour the light our parents gave us. They all gave us something, even the gift of being born. Using the Inner Child meditation and the journalling prompts which you will find in Chapter 10 will help you to start unpacking all of this. It will help you to let go of any fears and insecurities that have been passed down to you, and it will help you see that a lot of the heaviness you are carrying maybe isn't yours.

You can start to see that if you were someone who had inconsistent boundaries placed upon you, too much pressure put on you, or never felt you were enough—whatever it was, it is possible to undo the fabric of those lies and start to reparent yourself. This work can be confronting, but it can be so beautiful too. On the flip side, I had a lady who came along to my inner child women's circle who shared that she had a wonderful childhood, and somehow, lost that part of herself. She wanted to go back to a time when she was playful, brave, and excitable and have that lust for life once more. That was the first time that I witnessed such a thing, so please know if that is you, this work will help you connect with your inner child once more. As we close this chapter, I want to share something else I discovered about my childhood and my allergies. I want to touch on my childhood here because I feel it's important to give you some tools to help you in these moments to recognise the hurt inner child and to know how to help them.

My earliest memory is of primary school. I must have been about seven years old. We lived in a middle-class, small housing estate in the country in Wales. Within the estate was a school, so even from a young age, I would walk home. This was in the '80s, but I am still not sure if even back then I would have let a six-year-old walk home from school. Anyway, that is what happened, and I can't tell you the number of times I walked back to find my mother not home. I would knock on the next-door neighbour's door. Sometimes they were in and sometimes they weren't in. Sometimes I would play with the two sisters, and sometimes I would just sit and wait for my mum. My mum was a stay-at-home mum at this point in life and my dad a bank manager, so I not sure why she wasn't home on so many occasions. We lived in a cul-de-sac, and I would spend a lot of time with my friends playing, riding bikes, and having fun. This was the part of the '80s that I loved, that sense of freedom, which sadly so many kids don't have these days. There were no iPads, mobile phones, computer games, and life was about making fun. I am still so grateful for that side of my childhood.

My childhood memories in this home consist of lots of fighting and arguing, although that always seemed to be with my parents and my dad and half-brother and half-sister. I saw my half-brother kicked out at sixteen, and my half-sister was also kicked out at sixteen. My dad had adopted them when they were twelve and fourteen years old. He met my mum when she was 37, and they got serious pretty fast, moving in together, getting married, and then conceiving me in just twelve months. Even though they haven't spoken for over 25 years, I am so happy they met and had me, and am so grateful for this beautiful life that I have created. I have deep gratitude for all the storms and hardships, as it was in those times, I was able to find the light and learn all the lessons that my soul needed to learn. I feel that despite everything, my soul knew I needed to choose my parents, and I am so glad I did.

Feeling Alone as A Child

As I had shared before, my mum spent her days trying to save the world, writing letters to the local council and the government trying to change things in the world and smoking and drinking her way through life. Yet, in those moments, I feel she became so lost that she forgot to parent me. My dad was also a workaholic and wasn't home very much. When he was, he was very strict. His way was, 'Children should be seen and not heard'. If I had answered back to him, I would be given a mighty one! As I shared before, this was knickers down, across the knee and many spankings on the bottom with a rubber shoe.

On the flip side, it's so important to say that I had a great relationship with my dad. He would sing with me, bathe me, and read to me. He taught me the time, he would take me for new shoes, new clothes, and we would have dad and daughter days spending the time skipping along and singing. He had a beautiful side and through everything has always been there for me. I too followed suit and beat my brother and sister by leaving home at the tender age of fifteen, instead of being kicked out at sixteen. I have always been the change-maker, wanting to change the status quo and doing things my way. Many call it ADHD or Oppositional Defiance Disorder these days, but I call it 'strong-willed', so don't underestimate the power of these type of kids. They are here to change things, and if we can heal our inner child, we will be able to hold space for their determination and strong will so they can live out their lives' purpose here on earth.

My mum had a sweet side too, I remember her always baking and cooking and making everything from scratch. She would also make all my clothes and would have the most beautiful parties for me. I am sure she loved me, but I believe she had such dark demons that plagued her life, she was unable to cope without the bottle. My parents' relationship wasn't happy. I am not sure I ever saw them show love to each other.

Allergies In My Childhood

Throughout this book, I have tried to paint the picture of my childhood so we can understand the impact it has on children. I was plagued by allergies as a child. I was allergic to dust, dogs, cats, horses—all the animals that I loved—and had the most terrible hay fever, which would make summers hard. Even though I was so allergic to animals, we still had dogs and cats, and it does make me smile to think that my mother never linked my allergies with our animals. My hay fever was so bad that I remember pushing my face in a bowl of cold water, anything to make it stop. I used to go for horse riding lessons, and even with a mask, I wouldn't be able to see or breathe properly. I remember my dad saying, *'Susy, enough is enough. You can't go for any more lessons'*, which I totally understood.

I have since learned that looking at allergies from an emotional and spiritual element could be our body's way of protecting us. If I take my childhood as an example, your body feels an 'external threat' (my family's every day screaming matches). It releases cortisol (the stress hormone) which then produces histamine to support the 'external threat'. There is also evidence that supports that an anxious mother or an unsafe environment can cause such things such as eczema and even asthma. If we understand that stress can contribute to such allergies. *I wonder, did that happen to me? Was my body on such high alert that it produced too much cortisol and too much histamine, causing me to be allergic to everything and anything?*

Healing from The Inside

Three years ago, I met two amazing women who changed everything for Seren and me. I am so lucky they are based here in Perth, as they help parents and children from all over the world to heal such things as ADHD and anxiety. I say 'heal' here because I have seen this in both Seren and myself. Gone is the ever-distracted mind, brain fog, and anxiety, and what's left is still a dreamy, creative mind, and without medication can now easily fit into society and the schooling system. I believe when we 'heal' the body, the mind, and the emotional and spiritual self, no longer is ADHD a problem. It becomes merely a super-power and gives a person incredible confidence, creative abilities, and out-of-the-box thinking. There is nothing you cannot achieve when you can have this type of personality, which is why so many entrepreneurs, actors, musicians, artists, and inventors have ADHD. However, the medical world will make you believe that you and your child are broken and need fixing with medication. While I agree there are times when medication is necessary, we now live in a society that doesn't encourage healing the body. Instead, we move straight to medication.

When I met the nutritionist, Leigh, and the neuro-psychotherapist, Dr. Nat, I knew I was in good hands. My prayers had been answered, and they were exactly what I was searching for. Finally, someone wanted to heal the body from within and give me an exact blueprint of what was happening in both mine and Seren's body and mind.

Right before I started seeing Dr. Nat, I had been diagnosed with both ADHD and PMDD. The psychologist recommended a stimulant such as Ritalin for my ADHD and an anti-depressant for the PMDD. Dr. Nat explained to me that a stimulant given to an already over-stimulated body flooded with cortisol would have sent my anxiety through the roof. I knew I was never going to take medication. I knew there was a reason that was happening to me, and I was determined to heal my body naturally and not mask it with medication. If you remember, I had tried medication for both

> **Prayer is the medium of miracles.**
> **A Course in Miracles**

myself and Seren some years before. For us, I knew it wasn't the answer long-term and was determined to find another way.

Taking the Holistic Path

Instead, of taking the medication, I went a two-year path of healing holistically, emotionally and spiritually. Working with the nutritionist and Dr. Nat, they gave both Seren and I a QEEG brain scan (which isn't as scary as it sounds). Imagine a swimming cap with lots of wires coming out of it hooked up to a machine. The amazing thing is with this QEEG scan it can detect what's genuinely going with the brain and the body. This was the first accurate test that showed that Seren and I did have ADHD, bearing in mind I do not believe that ADHD is a disorder, merely a different type of brain with possibly more theta brainwaves than your average person. That means we are prone to daydreaming, but as recent data has shown us, daydreaming is good for us. We need more of it, not less of it. Scientific giants like Albert Einstein and literary masters like the Bronte sisters, to name just a few, were all gifted daydreamers. Setting their minds adrift led to their most towering creative achievements and aha moments.

The thing is, we are taught that we aren't supposed to daydream. How many little Jonnie's across the globe are told to stop daydreaming in school? Seren has been blessed with some incredible teachers who've said to me over the years that Seren either looks out of the window or draws when the teachers are talking. Each one would tell me that when they asked her what they said, she was able to recall all the information that the teacher had just said to the class. Just think how empowered our children would be if they were able to learn is this way. There is also a school near us that teaches some of the kids while they are bouncing on a trampoline. They understand that some of these kids have lower levels of dopamine and that exercise boosts our dopamine, helping us to concentrate. It seems like common sense to me!

Dr. Nat advised us that both Seren and I had higher levels of theta, and through something called neurofeedback, we could increase the other brain waves, therefore helping Seren to be more focused. One thing we did notice was that after just a few sessions, Seren was able to hold a full-on conversation about what she had done in her day. That never happened before, so for us, we saw a massive improvement in Seren's level of focus and concentration when engaging in conversation. The school told us they did not see any improvements. However, I feel that most schools don't allow for different types of learning and expect all kids to learn at the same rate. They are now also conditioned that medication is the only answer for ADHD, and I guess they didn't want more conversation from Seren; they wanted a quieter and more focused (aka drummed down) child. I have never been a teacher, so this is just my opinion, but my honest feeling is that if you have to medicate millions of children every day to fit into the culture of schooling, there is something very wrong with the whole idea of schooling.

Dr. Nat did, however, say she wasn't pleased with the results, and her instinct was telling her we needed to do further tests and investigate Seren's gut health, deficiencies, other such things like heavy metals, and change her diet. We needed to take out gluten, dairy, and only give Seren low-sugar while we put on her on a six-week protocol. Both Seren and I had a stool test, hair test, and further blood tests. The results showed that both of us had Group B strep present and not enough E. coli. They explained to me that with those levels of Group B strep, it could cause anxiety and ADHD symptoms! Plus, we had other gut health issues which meant that we needed to heal and repair the gut. The six-week protocol was easy, and even though Seren complained and had a few tears over the six weeks, she did it, and the changes were amazing! I have included the links in Chapter 10 to my Instagram live interview with the nutritionist, doctor, Seren, and me. If this resonates with you, I would love you to watch the video. These tests are not being given; instead, we are diagnosing children and adults with things they don't possibly even have! There are hundreds of reasons why we could be feeling anxious, lacking focus, or feeling depressed. Many of us now are so deficient in key nutrients and are swimming in a toxic soup, that it is hard for us to function as nature intended.

Living in Fight or Flight

It was Dr. Nat who discovered I had high levels of histamine in my body through the QEEG scan. I told her how that made sense as I had always had issues with allergies since being a child. She went on to describe that having that much histamine would only be generated by an increase in cortisol. My body would simply have to flush itself with cortisol (the flight or fight hormone), so my body could then have the histamine produced. That meant my body was constantly feeling an outside threat and putting itself in a constant fight or flight mode! She asked me how I was feeling, whether I was feeling anxious. I told her I was. It was so bad, and I lived with it each day and woke up with it. It was almost like I didn't know how to be any different. At that point, I started to cry as I knew it wasn't right to feel that way, but I also had no idea how to make it go away. I had previously been on antidepressants for five months, but it took me nine months to start to feel normal again. The medication helped me through a very dark time which I only share in my book, *The Diary of An ADHD Mum*, but I also have the insight to see that at the time I didn't have any other tools. That is one of the reasons that I want to share this.

Dr. Nat advised me that since being a child, my body had learned how to flood itself with cortisol, which could have been for two reasons. The first reason may have been to protect myself, as I have shared. The second reason may have been a response to my ADHD, dreamy brain. Maybe my body realised that to aid concentration, it could send a shot of cortisol and would continue to do this throughout the day. As Dr. Nat told me, '*Susy, no one can continue with this level of cortisol on their system. You will be heading for a nervous breakdown*'. That was three years ago, during my spiritual awakening, and I can tell you that when I was told these words, I left Dr. Nat's office and cried and cried.

I couldn't believe I had lived like that for all those years. I had hidden my anxiety from everyone, almost not acknowledging it and pretending it didn't exist, but it did, and it was getting stronger each day. Even on waking, I would feel so anxious that it felt as though I was peering over the edge of the cliff with my toes dangling into the wide-open wilderness. Yet, I was simply waking up from my sleep and putting on the kettle to make a cup of coffee. To think this level of anxiety was deep-rooted from childhood and was playing out through my body, affecting my mind and my hormones, was heartbreaking.

Healing Your Gut

I don't feel enough emphasis is given to how much we need to heal on the inside to support our brain function and our mental health. We know from so much research and data that our gut is, in fact, our second brain. Two thousand five hundred years ago, Hippocrates stated that all disease begins in the gut. Hippocrates was a Greek physician of the Age of Pericles, considered one of the most outstanding figures in the history of medicine. I do wonder how it is that we only realise the importance of his findings now. It's no secret that chemicals, pesticides, preservatives, vaccinations, heavy metals, and all other such things are affecting our gut microbiome and therefore, our mental health. It also affects our children, and we are now seeing a huge increase in mental health issues and diagnoses.

However, I also discovered from a healer that many children could have issues with allergies because of problems in their childhood. To me, that made complete sense. I had been trying to protect myself as a child. When I didn't feel safe, or my safety felt threatened, my body would flush with histamine. I truly believe this concept, and while I haven't been able to heal it completely, my allergies are much less than they were before. I have also not passed any allergies down to my children, which again I find fascinating. Even if we look at allergies such as childhood asthmas, we can often trace it back to the mothers and anxiety. There is so much more at play energetically than the medical world will give us credit for. We are so much more than our eyes can see, and there is an energetic field that is always at play.

Healing the inner child and writing this chapter has allowed me to see why I have such a yearning to live in the country. It has never left me. As a young child, I lived in the smallest of villages with only 60 houses, one shop, one pub and one school. I have such fond memories of that time. It was such a safe place to live, and even at eight years old, I would walk my miniature Yorkshire terrier, Boo-Boo, by myself. I remember my blue pinafore dress and pigtails, smiling and feeling so happy and at peace. Shortly after that time, my childhood took many different dark turns, as I have shared throughout this book. Maybe my subconscious wants to go back, replay the movie, take out the bad bits and make my life have a happy ending, but I have the happy ending right now at this moment. We can create it for ourselves; we can start over, and we can change our environment. I genuinely believe this.

Seeing the Gift Within

My intention for this book is to help you honour your pain and suffering, to allow you to bravely walk into the shadows, to learn to let go of what has happened and who you have been, and to know that your life can and will be brilliant. It is important that we dance with the shadows, heal our aching hearts, and then step into the light, never looking back, or at least being able to look back with compassion, forgiveness, and acceptance. Through healing my inner child, I have been able to make sense of everything that happened. I have been able to strengthen my relationship with Karl, with my children, my family, but also myself.

I have been able to allow myself to remember what happened, but also see the gift within, and to see that things happened to me so I could learn about forgiveness, compassion, and self-love. Connecting with little Susy had been so healing for me. For such a long time, I forgot who she was; she was overshadowed by guilt and the shame of my teenage years. By finally connecting with her once again, and holding her hand, I was able to step fully into my healing. I understand that for many, the inner child work can be confronting, so go easy on yourself. Take as long as you need and come back to this chapter and the meditations whenever you need to revisit your inner child. I have put some additional resources in Chapter 10 for trauma support should you need it. I am still working on parts of my inner child now, but with each lesson, I find another gift of healing! You got this!

CHAPTER 7
GUILT AND SHAME—IT'S TIME TO LET IT GO, SISTER!

Even though we're vastly different from the person we once were, the guilt and shame can linger around like a foul-smelling reminder of who we were. We need to fully accept this part of ourselves and trust that this was part of the grand plan. Once we lean into the shadows, we can let go and then truly be conscious in the present moment, connecting with our higher self—which is love.

I have shared so much with you in the book for two reasons. The first reason is that life is about stories, and they should always be told. Stories allow us to heal, connect, bind to each other throughout time and space, and to help us to ascend into our true self. The second reason is that I find writing one of the most healing and cathartic gifts. In my last book, *The Diary of An ADHD Mum*, I was able to discover so much about myself and my family through my writing. What began as a daily diary to help me with my isolation and loneliness trying to navigate the path of a mother with a spirited child became a poetic dance of the soul. I was able to discover so much about myself, and through this journey, I was able to find the jewel within—which was the work of *Heal The Mother, Heal The Child*. As the weeks, months and years followed, I never understood why I was called to do the work I was doing. Many see ADHD as a negative thing, but I have come to learn that if we allow ourselves to follow our impulsivity, it can lead us to the most amazing, vibrant, and heartfelt driven life.

Mistakes are merely learning and discovering who we are. Without mistakes, we do not grow; without risks, we will never appreciate how exciting life can be. Without breaking the rules, we never indeed find ourselves, and we get lost in the rules and regulations of life, which can be stifling for someone with ADHD. It is ok to do all the things, but the one thing we must let go of is guilt.

When I look back on my 43 years, there are some things that I probably wish I had never done, but then I wouldn't be who I am and where I am today. As I have shared before, my life has been very colourful, and I am so grateful I had my guardian angels watching over me, as I have needed them so much in this life. I am deeply thankful I have been blessed and lucky as I have put myself in some potentially dangerous situations in my life but always lived to tell the tale.

The universe sends you miracles in the most wondrous of ways.

Wishing I Was Someone Else

For so many years, in fact, probably most of my twenties, I used to wish I was a different person. My best friend of 25 years seemed to have it all when we were both 22 years old. She had an amazing, deeply committed boyfriend who was so in love with her. She had a great job, a top of the range of the sports car, and she and her boyfriend shared the most fantastic dream home. My best friend had a figure to die for and had the most fabulous designer wardrobe. What they had such a young age is what to us looked like the life of a footballer and his wife.

We used to call them the 'Posh and Becks' of the town. They were living the dream, and I so would have swapped my life with my best friend's in a heartbeat. The very next year, I was so lucky to find the man of my dreams, Karl, who is still my dream guy twenty years later. Our relationship has had its fair share of drama and ups and downs, but we are stronger than ever, and I am beyond grateful every day for that. My dad introduced me to the law of attraction when I was eighteen years old, and I am still to this day so grateful for that, as I have lived my life by it. He would give me cassette tapes from the gurus like Tony Robbins and Brian Tracey and I would listen to them in the car every day on repeat. Those valuable lessons that I learned have served me very well in life and at 22, single and miserable, I decided to manifest my dream guy. I met Karl days later. Thanks, Dad!

Karl had a great job and fantastic ambition. He had a knowing that he would be successful in life and worked hard to strive for that. I remember sitting in my best friend's dream home with Karl one day and saying how much I wanted what she had. At the time, we were heavily in debt, Karl had an old battered car, and we were lodging with friends, but he would tell me, 'Don't worry, Susy. I got this, trust me'. I didn't believe him for many more years and would instead hate myself for not achieving what my best friend had. It wasn't anything to do with what she had; it was merely a deep disconnect with myself. I didn't like myself and would have done anything to change and be someone different. I never told anyone that, but I hated myself. I couldn't see the gifts in front of me, which were my life, my friends, my family, and my soul mate Karl. I would keep externally seeking to see others as better than me. My confidence was so low that even a boob job, hair extensions, and extreme weight loss still never filled that void.

My lack of self-confidence continued into my thirties and only finally left me two years ago when I was 41 years old. It took that long, which is ridiculous, and I am so determined to teach my children to love and accept themselves. So far, with my almost thirteen-year-old daughter, it's working, and this makes me so happy!

Learning to Love Myself

The change for me came after reading a book called *You Can Heal Your Life*. I realised I had to let go of any negative feelings I had about myself. I also read a beautiful book about a near-death experience, and again, it highlighted to me the need to let go of guilt and shame about who I was. As I have mentioned before, my pre-programming was set to, *I am a failure*, or *I have let myself down*. It could apply to anything from dinner not working out as the recipe, not playing with my children enough that day, drinking too much alcohol (sometimes even just two glasses of wine), not going to the gym, or putting on weight. Sometimes even a bad hair day would make me believe I wasn't worthy and was a failure. I was so cruel to myself. I can't tell you how many times I have wished to be someone else.

From the outside, I am sure my life looked wonderful. People have always said to me that I was pretty with a lovely figure, yet I have spent my entire life thinking I was fat and ugly. I have finally let this go, but what a waste of negative thoughts for all those years. Thirty years of not loving me and being downright cruel to myself, which is why I am so passionate about teaching Seren to love herself, as that was frowned upon when I was younger. And let's be honest, I am not alone, right? *Am I sure you have been unkind to yourself too? Why do we women do this to ourselves?*

After understanding that our thoughts can negatively damage ourselves, causing such things as anxiety, depression, and even cancer; I knew I had to change my thoughts. I believe that so much of my dark thoughts came from my teens. I was a bit of a delinquent. I started experimenting with alcohol and smoking weed at thirteen; then at fourteen, I began to start with sexual exploration. By the time I was fifteen, I had left school and moved out of my home. Not only that, I unknowingly moved in with heroin addicts. To be honest, when editing this part of my book, I sat bolt upright and said out loud, 'You can't write that'. Of course, no one wants to share that part of themselves and be so honest and vulnerable, but that's what this book is about—shining the light on the shadows!

My Teenage Years

For so long, I hated this part of myself, the little teenage runaway who was so broken and trying somehow to find herself in the rebellion. But having done the work over the last few years, I hold no guilt or shame for this part of my life. I had been through such a lot as a child, and this behaviour was a way to find my tribe. There was very little support, love, or compassion at home. Home for me was a living hell, and I spent decades having nightmares about my last childhood home. That is why I hold in my heart the fact that if I can work on my healing, honour my children, and give them love, compassion, freedom, and will, they will be ok. I honestly believe that.

I was never allowed to be myself, I was never good enough, so I spent a lot of my teens trying to discover who the fuck I was—drugs, drink, and sexual exploration were ways to escape the bewilderment of my mind. I had an out of control mother and a very strict father, but the light in my life came through my step-mama, Cathy, and my baby brother Joe, who was born when I was sixteen. I am still so grateful they came into my life at a time when I was incredibly lost. My step-mum has always tried hard to step into the mother role, which I understand must have been challenging for her when I was an unruly teenager and she had only just met me! Even though my little brother and I are 16 years apart, we are still very close, and chat each week, which is so lovely. I am so grateful to these two humans for coming into my life, and the balance that they brought to our family.

As an adult, I feel at times I made some poor parenting choices. I have continued growing, learning, healing, and understanding that life is a journey, not a destination, and it's ok to make mistakes. I have stopped feeling guilty as it doesn't serve my children or me. I honestly believe one of the reasons my mother hasn't been able to have a relationship with me is that she is fuelled by guilt and shame. It's painful to sit with the guilt and shame of who you have been and allow yourself to feel those feelings. Just think how different our lives may have played out if our parents, grandparents, or someone else in the ancestral line had stopped running from themselves and instead lifted the veil and looked at themselves in the mirror.

Meeting and working with mums with spirited children, they always tell me they feel so guilty. Don't get me wrong—I felt the guilt for years. At times, it would consume me. It felt like a heavy cloud was hanging over both mine and Seren's heads. I felt it, and I am convinced she felt it too. I am not sure she even believed in me or respected me as the guilt was so heavy. Weirdly, I have been feeling guilt over Flynn, my adorable son, who is now six years old. I felt guilty that I don't remember much of his early years. I was swept up in a crazy haze of trying to navigate the journey with Seren and her diagnosis. There were so many appointments, meetings, and for eighteen months, it was never-ending. I felt a huge heaviness from family, who I knew didn't approve of the path we were taking with Seren, and again this brought up so much guilt and shame as a mother. Many parents who are struggling with their child can suffer from mental health issues too. The anguish of what's happening can be so hard to handle, and it can crush you.

Forgetting the Early Years

I don't honestly remember the first couple of years with Flynnie. I know I am so hard on myself and that I was a loving and compassionate mama, but I just wish I could remember those first two years. I feel moving to Australia when he was only three months old, and not having the support of my friends and family, put me in a sort of foggy haze where I was simply going through the motions of parenting but not even being present enough to remember it.

Despite all that, Flynnie is the most well-put-together little chap you ever did meet. Happy, charming, calm, intelligent—he is the most beautiful soul and the easiest of children. He is simply a dream to parent and is loved by teachers, family, and friends. However, I sometimes wonder if my desire for another child stems from my guilt over Flynnie. On the other hand, I have never stopped yearning for another baby. I simply never had that 'done' feeling others tell me about. If Karl said, 'Let's make a baby', I would be running for the bedroom in a heartbeat shouting, 'Take me now'! I can't tell you how many years I have prayed for an accident. Writing this book has allowed me to see that the door is still open to wanting to have another baby; the yearning has never left me. That is why this work is so important—you will never know who you truly are unless you heal.

Healing is the catalyst to your inner light—let it shine so you can see who you are.

I am still unpicking this part of myself to see whether it is about guilt or maybe lack as I feel I missed out on so much during the earlier years of Flynn's life. So, as I shared so much in this book, I will also be working through parts of the healing journey myself as I write these words to you. I want you to use your healing journal and start to write down all the things you feel guilty for. The Letting Go meditation will be so helpful for you during this chapter. Also, I would suggest journalling or even writing a letter to yourself. You could write a letter to your inner child or even your teenage self (yourself at any stage in your life, really), also later perhaps as a mother. Imagine you are writing to a friend who you love dearly. You see that they are struggling with shame and guilt, yet you don't see that about them, only their strength, love, and compassion. Write from your heart, not your head; you could put on one of the playlists I have given you in Chapter 10 and start free-flow writing. Let all the words flow onto the paper. It will be particularly helpful before doing the Letting Go meditation (trust me on this one). What's even more powerful is doing the exercise around the full moon. You can write the letter and then under the full moon burn the letter and let go of any guilt, shame, or negative attachments you have (I will be doing this tonight along with cleansing my crystals under the beautiful full moon).

Or you may want to listen to the meditation first and then begin to use your guided writing. There is no right or wrong way to do this, let your intuition guide you on which way is best, but honouring these shadows, shining the light on them, then burning them and letting the universe take them from you is so potent! I always find guided writing so powerful as, during the meditation, we connect with our higher consciousness. When we access this place, we bypass all the fear, conditioning, doubt, and judgment and step into the vessel of who we are. That is why so many times we can be moved by our meditations. There are so many times over the last couple of years in my healing journey that I have sat in meditation and sobbed.

Unblocking Our Chakras

I have felt so much guilt, fear, and sadness leave my heart, and I have felt my heart chakra begin to soften and open. Without us knowing it, our chakras have become so blocked, and when this happens, we are not truly at one with the universe or ourselves. When we start to heal and remove the debris, we allow more love to flow into ourselves. We are created from this thread, God, universe source, spirit or whatever word resonates with you; some call it the cosmos. It is there, and it is powerful and abundant and only wants us to have the most wonderful life. We are all destined for greatness, and this can start to happen when we allow that abundant flow to move through us. Again, in Chapter 10, I have given you some additional resources that have helped me on my healing journey.

The Chakra meditation can help you unblock these parts of yourself. Then you can start to find that you begin to share your truth, you begin to act and live only from the heart, you begin to be more present with yourself, your children, and the world around you. You can become more grounded and feel more secure. You aren't like a leaf blowing in the wind anymore, but instead like an old oak tree grounded into the earth. It's funny that as I am writing this now, I remember my dream. It was about lots of oak trees, and I felt so safe with them there. I also dreamt about a new baby and the old house we lived in before we left the UK. I have so many beautiful memories of that house.

Always be guided by your dreams and write them down in your *Heal The Mother Journal.* The dreams are here to bring us messages. I am now able to unpack mine, and I see the messages they have for me, but if you are unsure, you can grab yourself a dream book or search online. I get so many messages from my dreams. I honestly don't know what I would do without them. They will guide you through this process, as well as animals and creatures. Start to notice any animals, birds, or insects that keep coming into your life; our totem animals have messages for us. I have given you some extra resources for this in Chapter 10.

After you have written down the things that make you feel guilty or shameful, I want you to take each one and look at it and start to unpack it while using the word 'could' instead of 'should'. If I think back to Flynn and work on the guilt that I didn't play with him enough, I can use these words: *I should have played with Flynn more when he was a child. He was such an easy, self-sufficient baby, toddler, and child, but I should have sat with him playing more games. He was happily playing by himself, and I had time to work on my writing, but I feel like I should have had more playtime with him.*

I am going to swap those shameful words with more positive ones: *I could have played with Flynn more when he was a child, but he was so happy playing imaginary games by himself. I could have spent more one on one time with him, but he did his own thing, and he was happy. He was always very confident and self-assured, so I must have done something right!*

The first statement makes me feel so guilty. I don't think back to all the days hanging at the park or going to the zoo. I think of the times where I would write, and he would play with his Lego blocks. I think of the times where he would sit for a couple of hours playing Lego by himself, and I would happily work on my business or write my book. Because he was so self-sufficient, I would carry on. We would share some lunch, maybe head to the park, and then I would put a movie on for him while again I worked. I was honestly waiting for the day when he would start school and would feel such guilt about that too. Flynn didn't start full-time school until he was five and a half, but the girls started when they were four. He also refused to go to any type of playgroup, and he was so distraught I couldn't do it. So, he hung out with me, and together, we did our individual things.

Letting Go of Guilt

When I started to write this, the guilt was huge, yet coming back to editing it and having done the work throughout this book, the guilt has gone. I feel social media has a lot to answer for and can put a lot of stress on modern-day mamas. We see mothers with perfect houses, perfectly well-dressed and clean children, not to mention the whole family is dressed the same, even the parents—now that takes some coordination! The children never seem to watch TV or play electronics, and they spend their weekends making crafts, dens, or reading. But they won't show you the messy house, dirty kids, eating candy on iPads. They won't show you the mother having her tenth meltdown of the day. Many social media accounts are fugazi. In other words, it's whazy, it's woozy, it's fairy dust, and it doesn't exist. But also, for many of them, it is their business. Their brand sells, and they need to stay polished and shiny; the modern-day version of *The Truman Show* is now courtesy of Instagram. I am not knocking those mamas; they are rock stars! I only wish I could live my life like that, but that isn't me. It isn't my strength or my purpose in life, but it's theirs, and they are amazing! That is their gift, and they are letting it shine—good on them! But, if you are in any way holding onto guilt because your life doesn't look like that, then let that shit go, mama!!

It was such social media accounts that made me feel so guilty about Flynn. Instead of writing my book, I would have huge guilt pangs that I should be making a craft design from old leaves and pinecones. Then we should bake a pie with apples from my garden and sit down together, reading a book for hours. I am not suggesting that it isn't a thing, but it wasn't my thing. None of that came easy to me. I would spend hours playing crafts when Daisy and Seren were little, we would bake (still do), and I even used to sew with them, but that was that season. The season I grew into when Flynn was little was moving away from a full-time mum to be a full-time mum with a passion of my own. We should never feel guilty for who we are. Some mothers rock in all sorts of areas—find your strength, your golden flare and shine in that area.

Even though I felt I let Flynn down, remember those words have been deep-rooted, and I'd been saying them to myself since I was a child, but Flynnie is the coolest kid ever!! He is incredible and is the making of our family. He's super-intelligent, creative, plays instruments, loves reading, making Lego creations, and playing games like checkers and chess! Seriously, though, it is all within him, he is the driver of everything. He taught me to play checkers (yes, I know, right?), he asked to go to drum lessons when he was five years old, and now he's learning both the piano and the guitar. I now see why he is here. He is here to teach me to have less guilt and shame, to let it go, to teach me you do not have to give yourself entirely to your children, and you can still be the best mother ever, yet have time for you. It is possible.

And of course, this is more challenging when they are newborns and babies, of course; they need you. That stage I adore, I completely give myself to my baby and newborn. I cherish this time but don't forget to have time for you even within this stage. Ask for help when you need it, let others support you, and set your boundaries with your children and your partner—because you matter! Letting go of guilt is huge because when we don't have the guilt, we can set healthy boundaries. When we set healthy boundaries, we are triggered less. When we are triggered less, we enjoy life more and find magic within the mundane.

I had a lot of guilt over Seren. It was relentless, and to be honest, I still go through moments or seasons when we don't see eye to eye. I start to hear my mother's words come out of my mouth as I say unkind things to her. At times, I have almost shamed her into stopping a behaviour such as how she dresses (she doesn't dress like your average twelve-year-old), but again, it's me being triggered. I was never allowed to be myself, and even at thirteen, I was never allowed to put the tiniest bit of make-up on or remotely dress like a young woman or have my skirt shorter. I was shamed as a child for making those choices, and I have also found myself shaming Seren. But what is the root cause of all of this? Is it history repeating itself, or is it the fear of what others think, again coming back to place maybe when we a child and we were shamed? We don't want to feel that shame again in adulthood, so we repeat the cycle and pass the shame down the ancestral line. Seeing this, witnessing it and moving through it is why this work is so important. We are called to do this work to break the cycle, but trust that this journey isn't perfect. You will make mistakes, say things you regret, and pardon my French, fuck up, but don't get stuck here over guilt and shame. Keep moving forward, sister! *Never underestimate a cycle breaker. Not only did they experience years of generational trauma, but they stood in the face of trauma and fought to say, this ends with me. This is brave. This is powerful. This comes at a high cost.*

It's also been important to ensure that Seren doesn't hold onto guilt and shame from her younger childhood. Recently she said, 'But Mum, I am a bad child, and I always have been, this is the way I was made'. Straight away, I called her on it, and we worked through it. I shared how, when she was struggling, I was too, and a lot of what she felt probably came from me. I shared how I had made many mistakes, but together we had grown through them. I thanked her for all that she had done, as it was her behaviour that cracked me wide open. I reminded her that is why she came here, and I told her I loved her so much. She looked at me bewildered and then started to take selfies of her and me on her iPhone. Somehow in her almost thirteen-year-old brain, I think that was a moment of connection and understanding. I keep trying to drip feed her with the good stuff, helping her to release guilt and shame, so hopefully, soon a lot of that has been worked through her little soul. I don't want her to carry the guilt that she could be harbouring inside about her behaviour during her younger years.

By letting go of my guilt, shame, fear, conditioning and imprinting from my family, I was able to figure who I was exactly. I was finally beginning to learn to love me. I was able to have a deep love affair with myself for the first time in my life. I was able to learn to love the parts of me that before I thought were horrible. I was able to accept all parts of myself and find my truth. Life had never felt so good. It is from that place that we can start to have a deep, conscious and connected relationship with others around us. My marriage can strengthen, as Karl and I are no longer looking externally for that love; we have it within. We are not looking at our children as an extended version of others, but as separate and whole.

Our children do not define us; we define ourselves.

Our children feel the light and warmth inside of us, and they gravitate towards us. Friendships can strengthen, and others fall away as our new light is sometimes too bright for them. And our family relationships can become more robust as we honour our boundaries and work through our triggers. At other times, that relationship can drift like ships on the ocean but trust these seas, and the calm waters will come again. You will meet each other in the silence but with a new version of yourself. Trust the process.

We can often hold guilt in our cells, and we allow it to float around like a toxic soup while we repress things repeatedly—not based in love, but in guilt. I have friends here in Australia who return to the UK year after year. They had told me they feel guilty for leaving, and it makes their guilt feel less when they return home each year. I suggested that they swap the word should with could and then start to look at how that will feel.

Releasing Shame

What do you feel shameful about? What comes up for you when you think about it? Use your journal and let your words free flow. Maybe put on my Spotify playlist from Chapter 10 and without judgement write down anything that comes to you no matter how small or silly it may be—remember we are shining the light on the shadows and everything counts! We want to begin to release this from our cells, so it's important to be honest with yourself.

If I allow myself to think back, it takes me right to my childhood. How many times have you said to your kids, *'I am so ashamed of you'?* When I say it now, I cringe and retract straight away. Since I have become aware of the damage of this word, I no longer say it to my children. Can you see that when we say that to a person, it can lay a heavy burden on that person? If someone said it to me now, I would be devastated.

I am ashamed of you.

Gosh, it's brutal. You have done an act that is so shameful that someone would say that to you—shame is one of the worst things that can happen to a person. I once read that feeling shameful about yourself is so damaging, and it causes the worst type of mental health issues if we allow ourselves to carry that shame. We have all done something that we feel shameful about. But, to carry that burden not only affects us in this life but through epigenetics, it can run through families. We do not want to imprint this shame onto the next generations, so it's important we learn to let it go. As I have shared before, we can be holding onto emotions that aren't ours because they have been simply passed down to us. We don't have to carry our parent's shame, and the Letting Go meditation will be so helpful to release this. We do not need to hold onto our parent's shame and guilt; it is not our job. Remember that.

I am not a fan of the standard psychology route, but this is only my journey, I am not suggesting that everyone should feel the same way. I found that when I spent a few weeks with a psychologist, I felt like I was going mad. If you took me there now, it would confirm that they think I was mad! I feel that the psychology world does not always support the metaphysical world, and there isn't a way I could have carried on seeing my psychologist while going through my spiritual awakening. Can you imagine it? I might have been whisked off by men in white coats! There are indeed some fantastic, awakened metaphysical psychologists who can support you with this work. That is why I love Dr. Nicole; she is the biggest breath of fresh air that has ever been gifted to us. It is amazing to be able to learn, grow, and heal from such an incredible awakened psychologist via social media.

I feel that for me, one of the most profound healings for guilt, shame, the mother/father wound, and pretty much everything else, has been breathwork. I have mentioned breathwork a few times in this book and want to go deeper here and share more about this incredible healing modality. I have done breathwork sessions online, which were still amazing, but I have to say there is nothing more potent and healing than doing it in person. You can do it alone with a breath practitioner, or you can do it in a group. For me, the connection with others in this space is mind-blowing. I qualified as a breathwork teacher, and my training in Bali was undoubtedly one of the most incredible healing journeys of my life. If you feel called, I will recommend you find a teacher close to you. Again, I have shared some resources for you in Chapter 10.

Conscious Connected Breathwork

I was trained in the sacred breathwork method, also known as shamanic breathwork, holotropic breathwork, or conscious connected breath. Through conscious connected breathwork, we can enter a state of consciousness which is a state we get to when we deeply meditate. This meditation practise can take years to master, but the breathwork can take us to that place in just one session. The method I facilitate uses essential oils, sound, music, and ancient cleansing herbs such as Palo Santo and sage to take people lovingly to an altered state of mind.

In this state of consciousness, we can access our higher self and can bring forth incredible changes into our mind, body and spirit. I was able to heal my mother wounds on a deep cellular level and bring forth new clarity, understanding, and depth to my life. It changed me. I became a new person; in some ways, it was like a rebirth. The shamans have used this type of breath for centuries to heal and let go of trauma, but in the Western World we haven't been learning these skills, and so we pass on fear, trauma, and pain down to each generation. As I mentioned in previous chapters, animals know how to release trauma instinctively, yet we hold it in. Keep the stiff upper lip, shoulders back, carry on; we aren't taught to go to the pain and feel it, honour it, and allow it to heal us. We bury it, we push it away, and through that, we can suffer mentally and psychically with all sorts of pain.

Through conscious connected breathwork, which is usually done for around an hour, you can connect with other spirits outside of the physical plane. People may connect with those people they have lost, others connect with their spirit babies, or you may connect with your inner child. Some people do not connect with anyone but still, have a deep cathartic healing experience. Just imagine the gift we give to our bodies through breathing in beautiful oxygen deep into the lungs and body for an hour. We flood our cells with life—it truly is beautiful.

Through breathwork, I was able to connect with myself when I was in my mother's womb. I was able to feel the connection I had with my father and grandmother, but I could feel my mother's suffering. I will never know because we are not in contact, but I could feel she had postnatal depression and was indeed suffering a lot when I was born. I am pretty sure this was never addressed and maybe was the reason she went back to drinking. To be able to feel this through breathwork was very healing for me.

'The breath' in Latin means 'the spirit'. Our breath is our life force, and without it, we cannot exist. I discovered it is also our greatest healer when we use the breath through a conscious, connected movement. It is nothing to be feared; it is only our breath, our tool for healing, and it will only take us as deep as we are willing to go. Karl had his most significant transformation from breathwork. He was able to heal wounds that he didn't even know existed. He was able to release guilt, shame, and to finally let go of his father's guilt he'd been carrying since he was eleven years old. Sometimes we are harbouring and carrying guilt that isn't even ours—it can be passed down from generations. So many humans now realise that it wasn't the right time for their parent's generation to do this work, but as we collectively awaken, we start to awaken each other.

As I shared before, I love doing breathwork as a part group. When someone else releases which could be a shout, cry, or groan, this gives someone else permission to release too. It is incredible how much we are connected by our spirits and our energy. We are all connected, and we are all part of the universe and the divine energy of love. When we access this part of our subconscious together in a safe and held container, massive transformation can take place. If group breathwork isn't for you, you can also have private breathwork sessions. Breath is the bridge between reality and the spiritual realm, and it has been one of the most healing and profound journeys of my life. It is said that one deep cathartic breathwork journey is the equivalent of one year of psychotherapy. For me, I have been able to reach deep inside like a glove from the universe and take out the darkness and send it back to the light.

More Bubbling to The Surface

So much has come up for me writing this chapter. My spirited child has been triggering me, some of her old patterns have been coming up, I have found myself today feeling into that victimhood—*Why me? Why couldn't things have been different? Have I really caused all this to Seren, or is she just who she is?* Thoughts have been plaguing me today, and wherever you are in your journey, I want you to know that your child will be who they are supposed to be in this life. I am pretty sure my mother has her reasons for not having a relationship with me.

Maybe I triggered her? Perhaps she also saw a spirited child and couldn't deal with it? I will never know, but my wish for you with this book is to keep working on yourself. At times you can find as you begin the work, your child may play up, or their behaviour may seem worse. This has happened to me so many times, but I now see I am simply being tested by the universe to make sure that I am fully embodying these changes and this growth. Keep trusting, don't fall into victimhood—keep moving forth and continue with the work.

As you will read in this book, I am always changing my mind, continually growing, changing, ascending, and that's ok. I never regret anything. However, that doesn't mean I am not all over the place at times, and I want you to know that is life. It is supposed to messy and challenging and all over the place. As long as we keep going in the direction of the light and trust that as we pass through the darkness, that is how it is supposed to be. Sometimes I wonder what my life would have been like if I'd taken the traditional route, but I know I was never destined for that path, so with all the craziness and twists and turns (and I am sure there are many more to come), I love this life. It is sacred, and so is yours. When you walk your truth, you know that is the path for you.

Still Wanting Another Baby

It's funny that this book for me has brought up wanting a new baby. As you read in the other chapters, speaking my truth with Karl unearthed the possibility of having another baby. However, as you will read in this chapter, I was feeling that there was guilt and a yearning to have what I never had with Flynn as I was so preoccupied with Seren. During this time, I have also allowed myself to remember who I wanted to be, and that has brought up a lot of pain for me. At first, it brought happiness, remembering that I wanted to go back to teaching women about Hypnobirthing. I have had many moments in breathwork where I have clearly seen myself working with pregnant women through meditation and breathwork. I clearly saw their bellies, and I saw a sacred women's birthing cycles—I saw it all. I have wanted to go back to teach women about conscious conception, which is preparing your body for not only pregnancy but conception.

I wanted to teach women how to heal before they started to conceive. It was on my heart, yet my eldest daughter took me on a path I never expected. I guess if I am honest, there is sometimes still pain there I need to work through, but that's ok. I have the tools now, and I am open and ready to keep shedding back the layers. I trust that she had all these lessons to teach me first before I teach others. If it wasn't for my amazing daughter, I would never have understood the importance of healing before conception or known about removing toxins before conception. She has been my greatest teacher, but she had to be spirited, she had to be challenging, she had to have all of these different issues so I could discover how to heal her, but ultimately the gift she gave me, and the twist in the story, was that she healed me.

I wanted to share with you some huge things that have come up for me while writing this book. The first one which I have shared a lot is wanting to have another a baby; the second one is that I am putting my fears onto my eldest daughter. I wondered where this could come into this book, and it fits in here perfectly.

Running Away from The Memories

I have probably made some very selfish decisions in my life, but to be honest with you, they have probably been made from a place of guilt and shame. I wanted to run away from who I was and the places I had been when I felt shameful, such as my drunk driving offence. I wanted not to have to remember places where I would hang out as an unruly teenager. I wanted not to bump into an estranged family member. I have tried so hard to be different from some members of my family. I didn't want the reminder of who I once was, or who I even could have been. It haunted me. I needed to start afresh, and so many of my dear friends here in Australia are here for the same reasons. There are many reasons why we run—sometimes it's to run from ourselves, other times it's to find ourselves. However, what I discovered is that when you run, you still meet yourself there. You are not different, you are just in a different place, and the work still needs to be done. I needed to be in Australia to do the work. Running caused me to hit rock-bottom, but my soul knew this is exactly where I needed to be planted for the resurrection of myself to unfold.

I want to ask you now, and please use your journal to write your answer in free-flow writing style.

What is your soul yearning for?
What would you do if you knew you couldn't fail?
Who are you behind the mask?

Let the words flow onto the paper, don't judge them, just let them flow...

Rebirthing Myself

Over the last six years since landing my feet on Australian earth, I have rebirthed so many times. You may find with my writing that I go from spiritual and love and light to earthy and honest with a few F-bombs, but that pretty much sums me up. Sometimes I am meditating every day, doing channelled writing at 3 am and drinking cacao and green smoothies, and sometimes I am cursing, questioning, and hating my life!

Even with all the work, there is part of me still wishing I hadn't been such a delinquent and wondering why I was. *Was it because of my childhood, or was it that I hated school from the age of twelve? Did I hate school because of my crazy home life, and the fact that I was probably depressed and anxious, or would I have always been that way?* At age twelve, I found myself bullying other girls, which has been a big source of guilt for me. Was it because I was being bullied at home? Was I playing out my life towards others because of what was happening to me? They always say a bully has a lot of pain, shame, and suffering within. They often feel so unhappy with themselves that they bully others. It's funny; when Seren is bullied at school, we explore this theme. We talk about the other person, and we always discover that the other person is having issues at home or with their mental health. I have a lot of time for bullies, as when I was a bully, my home life was in turmoil. If we look deeper within the person, we may find they are the ones who need help and support.

My Younger Self

The two girls that I bullied seemed to have perfect lives—happy family, animals, horses, etc. I wanted to swap places with them in a heartbeat. Instead, I was mean to them, and it makes me sad thinking about it. Another time, one of the girls tried to kiss me. Instead of honouring the feeling (I mean come on, my teenage hormones were racing), I chose to tell everyone else that she tried to kiss me. I was really hiding the shame of people thinking that I was a lesbian. Gosh, it's such a confusing time, but I carried that guilt for a long time. People were so mean to her, and I was consenting. I should have been honest enough to take some of the blame for what happened. Her mum had suggested trying to learn to kiss with a good friend, she thought she could trust me, but when we were caught, I made out it was nothing to do with me. My memory is a bit sketchy on the details, but I do remember not wanting to feel the shame, so I allowed another person to take the rap! I could never have talked to my parents about this, so I found these challenging years incredibly confusing as I had no one to talk to.

One of the things that that came to me in a breathwork session yesterday was that I am putting my fear and guilt onto Seren. I am petrified of her going through the same things as me. I don't have these fears about Daisy and Flynn. I know and trust they will be ok and successful in life. I trust this with my heart. *But why don't I ever feel this with Seren?* Why don't I stop being so hard on myself and see I have done really well in my life and yes, while I didn't have the perfect upbringing, I have created the life I desired and have manifested it in own my life with my children and my husband. I need to be happy with this and realise I have done enough and be proud of myself. If this stuff can happen to me, and I can turn out well, why I am worrying so much about Seren?

I also realised it was time to stop putting those fears onto Seren and to keep loving her. She has been talking to me about wanting to change schools. She has been in a loving, supportive, new age-style community school for the last three years, but now the numbers have dropped, and she is currently the only girl in year seven. I know it's time for her to move schools possibly, but because of my relationships within the school, I am putting those fears onto her. I realised while writing this chapter that it was time to release all guilt, shame, and fear and trust in my child as my biggest teacher.

After the breathwork, which gave me some powerful insights, I was able to have an in-depth chat with Seren. We talked about her guilt and shame from when she was younger. We honoured it, we cried together, and I held her heart. I told her how loved she was, how much she had helped and healed me, and while she was spirited and strong-minded, I was so grateful she had chosen me. From this also came the understanding that she may want and need to change schools, and I am going to support her and trust her with that.

Letting Go of My Fears

Just because I had a tough time in school, it doesn't mean Seren will struggle. I must stop putting my fears on to her. It is time to listen to what she is saying, let the fear, guilt, and shame go and allow her to jump! I need to trust that she will find her wings on the way down and be held by life, just as I have been. I feel so much as parents that we want to protect our children from feeling the pain, but we must remember we need to let them make their mistakes and feel the pain; it is part of the process. We can't be afraid of the struggle, as it's often the struggle that makes us into who we are supposed to be in this life. We need to let our children go through the painful metamorphosis so they can be the butterfly nature intended. If you tried to help a butterfly to leave the cocoon, they would never be able to fly! The struggle from the cocoon pumps fluid into the wings giving them enough strength to fly. If the cocoon is cut open, the butterfly will live but will never be able to fly and live out its true destiny—the struggle is necessary. Sometimes we just need to get out of the way and trust the process as it unfolds.

As we close this chapter, I would love you to use the Letting Go guided meditation and learn to let go of these feelings that can hold us down and take us into a direction that isn't truly ours. I would love you to use your journal and write down what it is you want to release, then use the Cutting Chords meditation as an extra meditation if you need to. Keep using your daily future-self journalling as this will start to re-program your psyche and carve a way for the new you that is waiting for you!

CHAPTER 8

THE EGO AND THE INTUITION — A TALE OF TWO OPPOSITES.

There was a time when you needed your ego to keep you safe-guarded from the perils of life. She has served you well, and you love and honour that part of yourself. However, you are now growing, ascending, and awakening, and it is time to accept that your ego isn't allowed to be in the driving seat anymore. She may still travel in the car with you, but from now on your heart and intuition will lovingly guide you on your true path to enlightenment.

In this chapter, I will teach you how to know the difference between the ego and your intuition. The ego has played an important role in your life. She had kept you safe when you needed safety and a sense of belonging. At times, and for many women, our ego is now running the show, which is based on a false sense of security, and yet she is still trying so hard to keep us safe. We need to thank her lovingly for her wisdom and protection and assure her that she will always play a part in our lives, but it's so important that for the expansion to take place, we must lead with the heart. Once we can quiet the ego, we can start to live a life drenched in love. We can begin to parent and live from our heart space and tap into our intuition, instead of fear of the ego. I refer to the ego in this chapter as almost another person. I will explain shortly why I do that and why it has helped me to detach from my ego.

I am so excited to write this chapter, as knowing and under-standing my ego has been one of the biggest gifts of my adult life. My only regret is not knowing about this work sooner. I am still learning about this work, and as you start to develop your understanding, you can take it further and delve into books and resources that will help you. I love to keep it simple, so I will share with you everything that has helped and healed me and then give you further resources in Chapter 10.

I have shared quite a bit about Eckhart Tolle in this book, and I have touched on this work in the previous chapters. However, I want to share with you a story from Eckhart's book, *The Power of Now*, where he shared how he tried to take his own life. Eckhart was consumed by fear and anxiety, and he also shared how he had developed a considerable pain body from his parents, who were always fighting and arguing when he was a child. He also talked about how many of us are born with a tremendous pain body. I believe Seren was born with one of those, and I have shared that in my previous chapters. I feel Seren was carrying both mine and Karl's childhood trauma which played out in her behaviour. My intention for this book is to help you cleanse as much as you can from your body, emotions, and lineage so it is not passed down onto your child and generations to come.

Looking at The Ego

First, let's look at what we used to look at when it comes to the ego. Prior to Eckhart and all his incredible wisdom, we looked at the ego as the part of us that would be a show-off. You would hear people say, *Who does he think he is? He has such a big ego.* In some ways, that can be true. Many people live from their ego, but I have learned that is often because deep down they need healing and radical self-love. The ego is something they have built up to protect themselves. I believe so many people who act egoic deep down need an abundance of self-love and self-acceptance. The bravado protects them in some way from their true feelings and their shadows, and they probably don't even know this wounded part of them exists.

Eckhart has taught us that the ego is the wounded part of ourselves, often based on our childhood. He believes one of the most profound gifts we can give ourselves is to have an ego death, where we let go of 'I' and come back to the heart. For so long, my ego was running the show. I have shared with you before about our subconscious, the part of us that keeps us small and confined that is the ego. There was a time when I needed my ego to keep me safe, especially when I was a child and a teenager. However, even though I have outgrown that person, my ego is still louder than ever, although now I have learned to call her out and know when she is at play.

I once had a panic attack when I was driving on the freeway. It was nothing to do with the act of driving on the highway and was simply my life being frantic. I was super anxious, living on my adrenaline, and going through a massive spiritual awakening at age 29, yet I didn't realise it. I suppressed all my feelings and emotions and continued working and living at a million miles an hour. At that point, I was working 80 hours a week for a TV company in the UK. After another fifteen-hour day, while driving home at 11 pm, I had a panic attack. It was inevitable that it would happen at some point. That night became the catalyst to my fear of driving on freeways.

What Lies Beneath the Surface?

I have since realised that my driving fear didn't stem from that night on the motorway after a long day at work. It wasn't derived from my anxiety over a recent operation or being caught in the London bombs or that fact that I'd had a crazy year which had seen me leave Karl in London and move back in with my parents. Yes, I'd had a year of craziness, but often we look at stress and feel it's the reason why we started to have panic attacks or anxiety. What I discovered is that those stressful situations begin to unearth what is buried deep within. Sometimes something traumatic needs to happen to unearth what needs healing. As I have shared before, I feel that in the modern world, we try and label behaviours, medicate them, and wish them away instead of leaning in and trusting that this has come into our life for a reason.

What I discovered is that the ego is like our pre-programming and is here to protect us. Each time I would step into a car and head towards the freeway, my ego would kick in and almost scream at me to get off the freeway. She was trying to protect me as that was the place where I'd had the panic attack. Yet, as I have explained, it was so much more than that. However, I didn't understand the concept and so continued to struggle.

For over a decade, whenever I would go near the freeway, my ego would kick in again. Thoughts would whirl around my head—*it will happen again, you will go in to fight or flight mode, you will need to get off the freeway.*

When Our Pre-Programming Goes Haywire

The subconscious would be so loud that even though I was driving on the freeway, I would take the next turn off and use another route. This went on for years until I decided never ever to go on a freeway again, and I happily lived my life like that. There have been so many other instances in my life where my ego has stepped up and started almost shouting for me not to do something. My negative thoughts would drown out any positive thoughts I had. So, I would wilt, listen to my ego, and stop, shrinking in confidence and life.

There were times when my passion and my ADHD were so strong that it didn't matter how loud my ego would be—I would never listen. I knew in my heart and my intuition that path was for me. Even though my ego was strong and loud, I would listen to my heart. That didn't mean I didn't have hardships on my path. Yet, some of the most significant moments in my life have been walking the path of fire. It is sometimes necessary to get to the light—we cannot always go the easy way.

I knew if I kept listening to my ego—the voice of fear—I would never rise, I would never grow, and I would never become the strong, brave woman I was destined to be. I would retract into my shell, become weak, less confident, and play small at life. I believe none of us is here to play small. I think we are born for greatness, and when we strip away the ego, we can find that light within. I had this knowing that if I kept listening to my ego, I would become more and more insular. I would become more and more afraid. My ego had become Goliath, but it was time for me to become David and find my strength. I saw my mother's fear of driving on freeways become a fear of driving on any roads outside of her village. Eventually, she stopped driving, flying, or using any type of transport and became almost a prisoner on her own home.

Naming Glennis

One of the best suggestions I ever heard was to give my ego a name. I named mine 'Glennis', and she always shows up when I am making big life-changing decisions; 'Glennis' hates the strong side of me. She also comes up a lot when I worry about my parenting and when I address my fears. I had a deep knowing that I could never truly excel in all areas of my life if I had a fear of driving following me around like the grim reaper. I knew I had to release the fear and let my ego finally lay it to rest. After trying various types of self-help, I discovered psych-k, and this, for me, has been the quickest way to release this fear. One session later and now I am happily driving along the freeways. In fact, I have come to enjoy them. I have shared more about this in Chapter 10 for you.

On a recent very bumpy flight to Bali, I realised that even though I have done so much work, there is a still a part of my ego that needs healing when it comes to aeroplane travel. Remember what I said about my mum being scared of flying?

I never stepped on a plane until I was fourteen years old, and that was because of my mum's fear of flying. There are so many fears we are holding onto that are not even ours, and I have said many a time, that is why this work is so important—so we don't pass our fears onto our kids.

> When you shine the light on the darkness, it is no longer the dark. It is now illuminated, and when it is shining, it no longer becomes a fear. This is the part of our ego that dies.

The same can be said about so many things that our ego holds onto. As I shared, my dad and I had a little falling out, which was triggered by Seren. Something she did triggered him into remembering a time when I was a teenager. He was triggered, but for the first time, I was able to sit back and see it wasn't him, but merely his ego reacting to keep Seren safe. He went straight back to the time and acted based on fear from something that happened 28 years ago. Do you see how far back the ego remembers?

Repeating Old Patterns

I think about how many couples had split up when they were destined to be together because they simply didn't have the understanding or the tools to do the work. When Karl and I look back on our break-up, we both see that it was our ego that was in place. My ego was telling me that to be happy we needed to be like the others—have a house, car, mortgage, and be married with a baby, instead of coming from my heart-space, listening to my intuition, and trusting that our love was enough. I listened to my ego constantly without seeing the incredible gift, which was our deep love for each other. Karl too was coming from a place of ego and only listening to his head. He was so scared that what happened with his parents would happen to us. Instead of connecting with his intuition and trusting that we were soul mates, both of us allowed the ego to take over, and we ended the relationship.

Even now, as I write this, there is a pattern at home repeating, and I am still trying to work out where it is coming from, although I know it's rooted from my childhood. I am obsessed with keeping the house tidy, and Karl is the complete opposite—rather untidy and very laid back. I take on most of the roles in the house, and sometimes I get triggered and angry about that. When we sat down one day and started to chat about this, I began to remember my last childhood home. I remembered that when I was a teenager, our house was very untidy and dirty. My mum was lost and knee-deep in drinking, plus a costly and intense divorce with my dad, and she had no time for cooking or cleaning. I remember feeling embarrassed about the house; here comes that feeling of shame again, so for me, it's deep-rooted. I had nightmares about that house until only a few years ago, and even writing about this now I am getting *déjà vu*, which is always a sign you are on the right path!

I know my ego is trying to protect me. I almost have a silent mantra—if my house is clean, then I am not a failure. How silly this is! We are not on this earth to have a perfect home; we are here to have fun, live our lives, and be in the moment! And I know that when I leave this world, I am sure my final moments won't be spent worrying about how tidy and clean the house is kept. I know this based on my self-worth. If my house is tidy and clean, then I must be a 'good' mum. There is still so much I need to unpack around this, which I am doing, and writing this book is helping me so much, plus using all my tools.

Living in Our Egos

When I think back to my parents, they were both living in their egos. They spent thousands on their divorce, and they tried to hurt each as much as possible. Instead of coming from their heart space and letting go of resentment, blame, and ridicule, they were constantly reacting from their wounded egos. What a different world we would have if we all came from our heart space and not our egos. Recently when my dad and I had a small falling out, I was able to see that my dad's ego had been triggered. I emailed him, telling him I loved him, and I was grateful to him for being a great dad when I was younger. I was able to see it was his wounded ego at play. I didn't respond from my wounded ego. I simply left some space between us. I honoured my boundaries, and I began future-self journalling to help me move through it. I still believe what happened with my dad and me was a test from the universe. For the last year or so, I had been doing ego work and here was the test and lesson. I am so proud of myself on how I handled it. I didn't respond to the emails with anger and from my ego, but from love and compassion. My intuition knew my dad was being triggered, and he'd hurtled straight into the wounded ego, but he would never be able to acknowledge that or witness it. It was such a valuable lesson to be able to stand back and come from the heart. Such emails could have sparked an enormous family row, but I stayed grounded, honoured my boundaries, and let time take care of this for me.

My dad then sent me a lovely email saying he regretted sending the emails-this is from a man who's never said sorry in his life-so I was proud of him for that. I was able to let go of all that was said, even though it was about my teenage years. Such emails could have brought up my shame and guilt again, but I had done the work and could honour that part of me. I was able to see the person, the mother that I am today and not be triggered. Gosh, what a privilege to have done this work before the emails from my dad happened. I have since seen my dad, and instantly it was fine. He flew from England for a month-long holiday here with my step-mum, and we were able to sit down and have a good chat about it. He told me he was triggered by me writing this book. He felt I was putting the blame onto my childhood and not taking any responsibility for my actions. He didn't understand the work Karl and I had been doing, I think to him he saw it as 'woo-woo' and quite odd. However, when he saw the change in us as people and parents, my dad told us how proud of us he was. He couldn't believe the transformation in Karl and had so much love for us. My dad felt he'd tried his best when I was a child and a teenager and may have felt that I was pointing the finger at him. I assured him that there was no blame on my part, and I shared with him my feelings that we have probably existed in lifetimes before and were in each other's lives for a reason. My dad is so old school, but he always listens to me, and I have shared so much of my spiritual journey with him. Even though he doesn't understand it, he always says that to see us so happy as a family, it must be working. I finally feel like Karl and I have created the conscious family I always desired, and it makes my heart so warm and happy. I want you to know that if your parents get triggered when you begin your healing journey, stay grounded, send them love and compassion and keep doing the work.

Witnessing the Triggers

Start to have a look at some moments in your life when you have been triggered. Think back to the work that we did on triggers at the beginning of the book. Remember that the people that trigger us are in our life for a reason. They are our mirrors, and the trigger can take us to the unhealed wound. Allowing yourself to witness the trigger and begin to unpack it is where the work lies. From this place, you can start to set healthy boundaries, and you will begin to see your ego at work. You can call it out, as I do with 'Glennis,' and then come back to your intuition and your heart. That is where we can begin to live a more conscious life.

So, how do we fix this? How do we learn not to listen to our ego? Well, there are times in our life where our ego will keep us safe, and it has been there for a reason. I am thankful to my ego for its help in getting to me to this point, Yes, it definitely almost affected some friendships, even my relationships with Karl and my daughter Seren, but I got to a point where I had to stop listening to 'Glennis'. By now you will know that I am not your average person and that most people do not say out loud, 'Glennis, fuck off', but honestly, as soon as I say this, I instinctively feel 'Glennis' shrink and wither away. I hear a faint voice (my inner voice) say 'ok'. For years, 'Glennis' was very mean to me. The ego can also be described as our inner mean girl—the voice of doubt, the sound of fear, that voice that keeps us small and afraid. When we decide to answer the call and step up in our lives, we cannot keep listening to that voice. I hear my ego loudly when I am due on my period, but I am now able to hear my ego clearly and call her out.

For years, that voice would tell me I was too afraid, too ugly, too broken, too fat, too nervous, too all over the place. I listened for a very, very long time until one day I named and shamed her, and now we happily co-exist together, but with me in the driving seat! Look, there are times when we should absolutely feel fear. For example, if a tiger was chasing us down the road, or if we are standing next to a very busy road while holding your child's hands, I get it. I feel it too! However, there are times, and we are very much in these times right now, when we listen to our ego too much! We have become afraid of things we do not need to fear. The more we allow our inner 'Glennis' to become louder, the more we stop stretching and growing into the person we are destined to become.

Living as An Empath

We come to this world whole and pure, knowing our divine purpose on this earth, yet through conditioning, fear, and imprinting from our caregivers at home and at school we start to question our inner truth. We begin to become fearful of things; then when things happen to others, we can start to allow those fears to imprint us. I always said I could never be a psychologist because as soon as anyone would tell me their concerns, they would become mine. I am convinced that my crown chakra was wide open, and I would allow anyone's energies to permeate mine. If you are someone like that, it is worth understanding what it means to be an empath. An empath is someone who can take on things that are not theirs. You can struggle to watch the news, read the newspapers, watch horror movies or documentaries about crime, as you feel this pain deeply—it can send you into a spin!

It's also important to know and honour yourself. Empaths can also get upset and intuitively know when people aren't telling the truth, and that can be a big trigger for them. You can also struggle with fake conversations and anything of a low vibration. If you are in a conversation with someone and it starts to become toxic about someone else, check-in with how you feel. Don't get me wrong; I am a woman, and for many women, we are partial to the odd gossip. I see it with Seren, and I am now teaching her and giving her tools on how not get drawn into those conversations. Whenever I start to engage in such discussions, and it doesn't feel right to me, I change the conversation.

Our ego has a good time blaming, judging, and being unkind about others. The ego feeds off it and can start to make us feel better as we put down another person. However, our intuition knows that isn't right. Whenever I see or feel someone being unkind or bullying others, I always feel it's because they have low self-worth, and they lack in nurture and self-love for themselves.

If it doesn't feel right for you when you get into a toxic conversation with someone, simply change the conversation or gently remove yourself from the conversation. Practising honouring boundaries allows you to be brave enough to tell that person openly and honestly that while you love and respect them, you don't wish to engage in that type of conversation with them anymore. It takes a lot to do that, but you will find that you will help them so much as they will start to witness this toxic approach only lowers their vibrations.

Our aim in life is to raise our vibration to love; that is where the magic lies.

Honouring Who You Are

As an empath, I also discovered that I struggle with arguing and fighting, and I have found it more difficult as I have started to do the ego work. I have found I don't generally like crowds and never have. The medical world will have all sorts of diagnoses for it. I have learned I can almost suck everyone's energies in like a vacuum, and it can make me feel heavy, tired, and low. I don't enjoy going to bars or clubs; it could be my age, but again, if the energy is low and I feel it, it can make me feel anxious. For so long, I would drink to feel comfortable in those situations instead of being sober and allowing myself to feel it isn't for me. I have had conversations with friends about this too; I explained that I love them, and it's nothing to do with them, but it wasn't for me. For so long, I just did what I thought I needed to do. I wanted to make others happy and like me, but I came to learn that I wasn't living in love with my life. Now, I only do things that feel in alignment. For me, that is family, women's circles, healing circles, and community events and connections not based on alcohol but love and connection. I have been able to manifest these friendships and people into my life when I started to honour and listen to my intuition and come back to my heart.

I want you to learn to honour your intuition, as when you start to lean into her and listen, she will begin to become your most powerful tool as a woman and mother. When I was going through the diagnosis stage with Seren, I met so many experts who did not feel congruent with me. I would listen to their words, I would watch their actions, and inside my intuition was screaming, *Do not trust them!* but my head and my ego were listening to them. That happened because I was so out of alignment. I was homesick, lonely, and possibly suffering from undiagnosed PND brought on by such a massive move when my little Flynn was only three months old. Karl and I were in a completely different place. I wanted to be with my little family and cultivate my new life in Australia, and Karl was trying to find himself as he stepped away from the corporate world that was all he'd known since he was eighteen years old. Suddenly, he was immersed in my life of feeding, nappy changing, and looking after babies, and he loathed it. To find himself, he went on lots of different solo trips, and the more he went away, the more I began to drown.

Listening To Fear

I was drowning, and when you are drowning, you make poor decisions. Funny enough, I had recurrent dreams about drowning back then and didn't realise. That is why it is so essential to understand your dreams, and always do your research on your dream, as they have messages from your higher self. I wasn't listening to my intuition. She was trying to reach me even in my dreams. I could hear her soft whispers, but I would shut them down and only listen to my ego. My ego was full of fear, and I believe that is why I trusted the experts. I didn't trust my intuition, and I let her whispers be drowned out by my ego. If only I knew about 'Glennis' then!

The more we listen to fear, the more fear is attracted to us. We put out this energy of lack, fear, and scarcity, and so the universe brings it back to us. Manifesting isn't just about getting what we want through our thoughts, actions, and beliefs. We can also bring in and manifest precisely what we don't want by thinking about it, so it's important that you are clear with the universe!

If you are in a place in your life when you know that fear is driving the show and your ego is making the decisions; it is time to let this go and start to walk a new path. You will need courage, faith, and trust, but I guarantee if you begin to walk this path and bravely put one foot

Fear is the lowest vibration and doesn't serve humanity. Love is the answer we seek.

in front of the other, your life and relationships will change in so many miraculous ways. One of the best ways to stop listening to the ego and start listening to your intuition is to take these steps, as below. I have given examples here, as well, to help these steps land for you.

1. **Detach yourself from people who bring you back into the ego and a state of fear.**
   I had many of these people around me when I was going through the journey with my daughter. These

people ranged from family and friends to experts and teachers. While they all meant well, and I respected their opinions, I needed to move away from them, as it became so noisy. Thoughts like, *Well, they all think the same. They all think we should medicate, so maybe I am doing the right thing. They clearly know what they are doing, so I must listen to them.* My intuition knew the answers. She knew I needed to get a better connection with my daughter. She knew my daughter was feeling lonely, isolated, and unloved, but I didn't trust her. I didn't trust me, so my ego won—my fear won until one day I found the strength to listen to the whisper. When I finally did, her voice became a roar!

2. **Stop reading or listening to anything that pulls you back into your ego and that fear state.**
   If you are reading something and deep within you feel fearful or uncomfortable, know you should move away from it. I now get this with trashy online newspapers (yes, I have a penchant for reading *The Daily Mail*). As soon as I do, I feel itchy inside, almost anxious. That stuff feeds our fear and lowers our vibration. It's the same with books about ADHD. I can't read them. Remember, we will never change and grow as a society if we keep listening to everyone else's ideas. We become stuck and stagnant, and that isn't spiritual growth. *Trust your instincts and let go of logic. Dare yourself to go against the masses.*

3. **Hold your heart with your hand and ask her the question instead of listening to your head.**
   Try this instead of listening to your monkey brain with all its fears and egoic ways. When I have questions or I am at crossroads, I will hold my heart with my hand, take some nice, slow, deep breaths, close my eyes, and ground myself with my bare feet on the floor. Then I ask my question, and I hear the answer loud and clear. Your heart is like your second brain but

way more powerful. She holds all the answers, as she is connected with the true source—the source of love. *Trust her, always.*

4. **Remember your ego will keep trying to pull you back to fear and lack.**
   When you have heard your heart's answers, your ego will try to talk you out of your decisions. Your inner 'Glennis' will bring back all those fearful stories others have told you over the years. Suddenly, that newspaper article you once read or the documentary on TV will come back to you, and you will start to question yourself. It can truly be a battle in your mind but trust your heart as she has the answers, and she is never wrong. I have never made a poor choice from listening to my heart. Our freedom in this life is to feel, embody, and understand love. God is made from this source, as is the universe. It's all made of love. It is the most potent force in the cosmos. You are connected to this source; you just need to trust it. Remove your mask, take off your egoic cloak, and step into your truth.

5. **Use the guided meditation to cut cords with your ego and start to live your life from your heart space, which is your intuition.**
   Most of the time, my intuition brings me back to love, but sometimes it can bring me back to fear-based feelings. I must check in with her and check that it is not my ego. It is so important that I am only feeling into my feelings and not that of others. There was a time recently on our road trip when a campsite did not feel right for me. I wondered if it was my ego (keeping me safe) or my intuition. I asked my heart, and she told me straight away that it was right to leave. I told Karl that we needed to go. Usually, he would have told me not to be silly, but this time he could also feel the energy and agreed we needed to go. We left very quickly and then headed up the

mountain for what seemed like an eternity. We got so high that we were amongst the clouds and the drop at the side of the edge of the road was making us all go queasy. However, we trusted. I had felt my intuition speak loudly to me, so I let go of all logic and onward we went. We eventually got to the top of the mountain and found the most idyllic sweet town and spent three glorious days up there. The locals were wonderful. We spent days in the forest, swam in the most beautiful waterfalls, and cooked marshmallows around the campfire. Even though I had felt fear, my intuition was trying to take us to a place that was just perfect. I feel that my intuition is connected to my higher self, and my guides are trying to help me, guide me, and keep me safe. Trust those inner niggles. They are nearly always right.

6. **Remember to call-out your inner Glennis!**
   If you have thoughts that you are not good enough, or even worse, thoughts that are unkind about yourself, know that is your ego. Using the Cutting Chords meditation and doing some work on your inner child will help you so much. Around my moon time, I spoke to myself in the cruellest way. Now, when I hear her faint whispers that I am a failure or I am not worthy, I call her out. 'Glennis shut up'! Honestly, I feel her wither and crawl under a rock. The work I have done over the last few years has healed me beyond anything I could have ever comprehended. I have learned to love and truly accept myself, and from this place, my vibration is higher than ever. Yes, there are always going to be things I wish to change, but I am me in this body in this time, and I will use my gifts well.

7. **Let go of all comparison and learn to love yourself.**
   I had a Post-It® note on my mirror for months that said, 'I am enough'. I would tell myself all the beautiful things about me in the shower, and I would be

kind to myself. When was the last time (if ever) that you kissed your hand and said to yourself that you loved you? Do it now. Kiss your hand, arms, shoulders, and say thank you! We will be diving into this subject more in the next chapter. As we learn to heal and let go, we create more space for self-love, and this is truly where the fun starts! The beautiful thing about this is that I can teach my beautiful children now that I know how to love and accept myself and listen to my intuition over my ego. I hope by now you are seeing the important and potent work of healing the mama to heal the child.

The Law of Attraction

As I shared before, my self-help journey started at the tender age of eighteen when my dad gave me some Brian Tracey tape cassettes. I listened to them in my little red Fiat Panda car. I seriously felt like Noddy in that thing. I would listen for hours on end about the law of serendipity, the law of attraction, and how we reap what we sow. I learned so much, yet in many ways, I needed to go through many life lessons to understand and fully comprehend the experiences related to these tapes. The main thing I learned was the law of attraction and how powerful the universe is. I have since read and studied many other books about manifesting and the universe, and I put them into practise each day. I have got to the point where I am unable to say anything negative because I truly believe in the power of our words, actions and intentions. Karl and I discovered twelve months ago that when we started to talk about negativity we could bring into our lives. We witnessed this, and now we both try to refrain as much as possible from talking about negativity, labelling events, or catastrophising things. Whenever I have a negative thought—I will say out loud, 'Delete that thought'. I learned that from a backpacker years ago when we are travelling around Western Australia, and it has served me very well in life. We don't want our ego putting out negativity into the universe when we understand the power we have to co-create our future. It serves no purpose whatsoever to talk about negativity. I know there will be a time when you want to have a bloody good moan—after all, we are women, right? I do this, too, but I would say now is that I try hard to live most of the time in positivity, not negativity. When we genuinely understand that thoughts become things, we begin to live our lives from a completely different place.

Right now, I am 43 years old, and even though I don't look or act my age, my ego is questioning whether we can have another baby. I have wanted another baby for so long. My days are busy with my writing, women circles, and my gorgeous family, but this yearning has never gone as I have shared with you in this book. It's funny as writing this book and doing the work has given me permission and given me a space for allowing these feelings to come to the surface. I feel like I have shined the light on these shadows and honoured them for the first time in years.

Downloads from The Universe

Almost twelve months ago, I started waking at 3 am and receiving downloads from my guides. I have always practised guided writing, and I recommend that everyone does it as a way of connecting with our higher selves. Guided writing is when you meditate and next to you have a piece of paper with 'Guided Writing' written at the top. After the meditation, you start to write and allow whatever needs to flow onto the paper. Write without judgment, as you will start to feel your ego popping up, but simply ignore her and continue writing. I had been doing this for about three years when I began waking in the night to different frequencies I could hear in the room. The frequencies were not in my ears, and no-one else could hear them, but through guidance from a very good spiritual friend of mine, she told me to use my angel cards and start to write. I will be sharing a lot more of this in the future and designing angel cards to share all the beautiful words that flowed through me. The downloads were the catalysts of both Karl and me going through a massive awakening.

There were many messages for Karl and me, and when we acted on them, the most amazing things started to happen. Karl ended up travelling to some of the most amazing places and meeting the people he'd wanted to meet his entire life. He created a worldwide app called Awaken and began living his life from a whole different place.

The reason I am sharing this with you is that my ego has questioned this so many times. I'd hear that inner voice of doubt say, *You are making this up*. 'Glennis' tries to keep me small, keep me afraid, and the inner-mean girl almost pulled me away from doing this work, yet trusting and going with it has changed our lives in the most supernatural way.

Even sharing this with you now, I start to feel uncomfortable, but I know it's so important to go first, to share my truth with you so you can begin to live out your life's purpose, whatever that might be. All the messages were written in a way I do not write. Some of the words Karl would need to describe for me. Often, I had no idea what the messages meant, but when we researched them, the hairs stood up on the back of our necks. We would get full-body goosebumps as we realised the writings were some of the most profound teachings ever. I honestly had no idea how I would know this information. Other times, I would write messages for Karl, and he would be blown away as there was no way that I would know this information. It truly was such an incredible time for us both. I genuinely believe I am connecting with both mine and Karl's guides, as I hear different frequencies when it happens. I have guidance about our health, our future, children, and a future child. It is extraordinary how it started to happen. For a time, I wanted to shun it, but I continued to ignore my ego and always came back to my intuition. I trusted the journey, and all that was unravelling.

During this time, I started to connect with my guides on a nearly daily basis. I began to ask them for signs about whether I would have another baby. I asked them to play a particular song, and twice I heard the song in different places on our travels, although this song is twenty years old. Again, I asked for a sign I would be having another baby, and a blue baby's sock landed in our washing pile. That has never happened before, and we have no idea how this cute baby boy sock fell into our washing pile while travelling across Australia, but it arrived that very next morning after I asked for a sign. If I listened to 'Glennis', none of this fantastic stuff would have happened to me, so sometimes we really do need to let go of logic and trust!

> Don't move the way fear makes you move. Move the way love makes you move
> - Rumi

Asking My Heart The Question

When I soften myself and hold my heart, I ask her, 'Should we have another baby'? The answer is always 'yes', and even though 'Glennis' keeps rocking up 'don't do it', I keep checking in with my heart and my intuition, and it's a firm yes! In my breathwork the other day, I had a clear knowing that this baby would be more for Seren—to help her heal—than it is for me. This baby would be our missing jigsaw piece. So, I am excited to see what happens for us and whether another baby will bless our family. This has been the most profound lesson for me, to stop listening to fear and the wounded ego and instead connect with my intuition and live my life from this place. When I shared my desire to have another baby with some friends and family, they started to tell me how they also wanted another baby, but they never did because of worrying about their age, money, the size of their house, their career, etc. But deep down they wished they had done it too (the thing is they still can). Some of my friends have wanted to travel more, go backpacking, change their career, but then fear and self-doubt would pop up. Can you imagine the lives we could lead if we stopped listening to our inner Glennis and lived from our heart space and our intuition?

As I close, I want to share something my friend said to me when I shared my desire for having a fourth baby at age 43. She told me, '*Crazy means unique sprinkled with stardust and soul alignment. It means following your heart and aligning your head to follow. Crazy means a dash of different with a pinch of "I live my life my way", so I can give others permission to live their lives the way they want, as well*'.

When we stop listening to our ego, and we start listening to our heart, we truly can have the most magical life—and that is my wish for you!

CHAPTER 9
LIVE YOUR LIFE YOUR WAY, GIRL!

'What others think of me is none of my business'. This has now become my mantra, and I will always carry it in my heart. How many of us are truly living our lives and how many of us are living lives so we don't upset others? When we start to put boundaries in place, we can also start to let go of other's expectations of us. It is from this place we can start to live our very own joy-filled life, free of guilt, and fully embodied in our truth.

Are you really living your life in a way that feels congruent to your soul, or are you living your life how you think it should be lived?

One of the biggest regrets people have on their deathbeds is that they didn't live their lives. We only have this time in this body in this life, and it's important we make it count. This chapter will help you to let go and release the burden of what others think of you so you can start to live your life. When we get to this space, we can truly feel joy, and it is a beautiful space to be as we then attract more joy into our lives.

As we embark on the last chapter together, I have taken you on a journey of shining the light on the shadows, letting go, and healing. As we come to the final chapter, it is so important you now call forth all you seek for yourself. I once read that you should write a book for what you need as what you need will serve others. I hadn't realised until I wrote this book how much guilt I had been holding on to and how much I needed to heal. Also, speaking my truth was a massive thing for me, as I worked through the chapters on triggers and boundaries. I never expected this book to bring about a small falling out with my pops, but again, that is what needed to happen. My relationship with my children, especially Seren, is now amazing (well most of the time). The bond with Karl has been strengthened, and it's all happened as I have been writing and editing this book. Life isn't always hearts and rainbows, and while writing and editing this book there has been a lot of turmoil happening both at home and in the world, but I have stayed faithful to my practise and my healing, and that has served me so well. It's interesting that I have been editing this book during a worldwide health crisis. I feel that so much has been happening physically, emotionally, and spiritually. I am forever grateful as this book has kept me in the work, especially being able to let go of guilt and shame as these last six months for humans collectively have been profound. This has been a considerable time for the planet to have to sit with ourselves and discover who we truly are, many of us awakened through this time, but I feel there is much more to come from this time on earth together.

I feel like we have been on such a journey together, and I want to thank you so much for being on this ride with me. I have shared some of my deepest, darkest fears, and have openly shared things with you that I have only ever shared with Karl and maybe two other humans. I have also shared some of my biggest dreams and desires with you, and I hope that through my sharing, it has unearthed something in you. I want you to live your very best version of yourself, to be able to strip away and let go of all the debris, to crack the shell on the rock, and to discover your inner diamond waiting there for you. I know you are ready to let yourself sparkle and shine out to the world. There has never been a better time to do that. As our planet begins to shed the darkness and shines the light on the shadows, it is a potent and incredible time to do this work as a collective. Many doors are closing for us, but together we must hold trust and reverence that there is a greater force at play.

Unearthing the Real You

Through this unearthing of self, we fill in the darkness with light. We come back to our truth, to our divine birthright, and to this powerful time. I am so excited for you as you begin your healing journey—now is your divine time. Now is your time to be activated, and whatever brought you here, I am so glad you came home.

In Chapter 10, I have included some prayers, meditations, healing tools, and other resources to help you to heal at each stage of your journey. I have also added music playlists and songs to help your heart chakra burst wide open. As you know by now, my intention and my dream for you is that you will heal not only your wounds but ancestral wounds. Once you heal, your body is lighter, and your heart chakra expands and allows in more love, more joy, more compassion, and more abundance. You can finally become the person you were destined to be when you arrived here on planet earth.

By now, you will know the difference between your ego and your intuition. I find that my intuition is based in soft, gentle nudges; at other times, it's a deep knowing. Whereas my ego is loud and bossy and isn't congruent with my heart and higher self, instead she is full of conditioning and imprinting from my childhood. Holding that in your heart, I want to grab your *Heal The Mother Journal* and write at the top of the page, *The (insert your name here) Manifesto*. So, for example, mine would say *The Susy O'Hare Manifesto*. Then I want you to write down your dream biography. You are going to be writing everything down as if it's already yours and has already happened.

For example, what you have achieved—your life, your career, your family—write it all down and let your intuition and your heart flow. Do not let your inner 'Glennis' stop you from writing anything, just write it down. You must imagine your dream life, and how you would write your biography. Let the magic flow. Don't hold back in any way. Think about your partner or your marriage, or the partner and marriage you want. Think about your children or what you want your children to be like. Think about where you want them to go to school. Write down everything. Let it flow, girl, and do not hold back. Put on one of my Spotify playlists and have fun with it. Even write down about your body, your home, your health, your happiness—write each one down and let it flow. Dream big, my friend. Remember, everything is possible when allowing the energy of the universe to pass through you. Remember, you want to write this as if it's already yours—that's the beauty of this. And so, it is.

Next, I want you to write down at the top of the page, *The (insert your name) Gratitude Journal.* Then I want you to write down everything you are grateful for in this life. It doesn't matter how big or how small; simply write it down. When was the last time you thanked the smallest things, such as waking up in the morning, the gift of your eyes, or your legs that carry you? It's all the seemingly little things we take for granted that give us the experience of life as we know it here on earth.

Magic in The Mundane

This morning, my beautiful boy Flynn came into the kitchen at 5:30 am as I was writing this part of my book. He was so sleepy and gorgeous, and I lay him down next to me on the sofa and wrapped my woollen cardigan around him. Within minutes, he fell back asleep. I found myself staring at him—his beautiful little face, his gorgeous blonde hair. I held my heart and said, 'Thank you'. I am so grateful every day for this little chap. He has been the easiest of children, and I am eternally grateful that he blessed our little family. *Think of all the things you are thankful for and allow your heart to show you.* You will be surprised what pops up. Again, let it flow sister! One of the most powerful things you can do to support your mental health is to practise daily gratitude. You can interrupt any negative feeling with gratitude. It really can make a huge difference.

I always remember when I was going through a tough time after we arrived in Australia. I had a little stand in the kitchen with daily quotations on it. You could change them each day, and I remember one day looking at the card on the stand. It read, *'Today I am excited about everything'*. As I looked at it, I started to cry. I remember saying, 'But I am not excited about anything! Not one little thing'. This was months before my healing journey began. I had no tools to help me whatsoever. I had three beautiful children, yet I couldn't see the gift in front of me as I was so in my head. Shortly after that, as I have shared, I went through a massive awakening (disguised as a breakdown), and my life has never looked the same since. Trust your journey and all its unravelling. I now try and practise daily gratitude even in those small moments like I had with Flynn today. It's not always me writing things down, but I now stop and appreciate the smallest of miracles, as one day those will be the things that I miss the most—even those mucky little handprints on my clean windows! We can become so busy, but always try when you feel overwhelmed or stressed to stop and look at the sky. Look at the birds, watch the trees sway in the wind, and remember who the fuck you are! You are an amazing miracle, and the chance of you even being born is one in a hundred million! Let that land! I came across the poem called 'The Butterfly Effect' and wanted to share it with you—I want you to remember how amazing you are!

The Butterfly Effect

You need to stay. And you need to stay loudly. You're afraid of making bad choices, but the truth is that the tiniest actions will influence the course of your life, and you cannot control it. So many factors play a part in you being here today: a delayed train, an extra cup of tea, the number of seconds your parents took to cross the street. This is chaos theory. Sensitivity. Mathematics. You are here, and every choice you have ever made has led you here right now, reading this. While you exist, every movement and moment matters; those bad choices led you to the best days of your life, if you were to play rewind. So, let them go. Change will come even if you're standing still. Butterflies will keep flapping their wings and causing hurricanes. So, make your choices and make them loudly. Trust your gut. Trust your energy. And if you ceased to exist? Oh, the universe would notice. The mess that would make. The hearts that would break. So, stay. Stay for bad choices. Stay for great ones. Stay. Cause a few hurricanes. ~ SRW Poetry

Life Isn't Perfect

I am a mother of three (hoping to be four soon!) Life is crazy and messy and imperfect, but I am learning it's these crazy moments that make up the very fabric of our life. Those are the moments we will remember; not how perfect our life was. I always remember travelling along with Karl and the kids in one of my favourite places in Australia called Byron Bay. The car windows were open, the wind was blowing around us all, the sun was shining, and the artist Xavier Rudd was playing 'Follow the Sun' on the radio. Karl looked at me and said, 'This is it. Right here at this moment, this it. It doesn't get any better than this; this right now is it. This is the moment of bliss'. That memory has always stayed with me. There wasn't anything specific that happened at that moment, but we both stopped and appreciated life and the wonder that it can bring us when we allow ourselves to feel into the moment, instead of always looking ahead for more.

One of the greatest things I have learned is that we are all chasing the unicorn and the fairy tale. We believe that at the end of the rainbow is a pot of gold instead of seeing the rainbow right in front of us. We are looking for the magical unicorn instead of seeing that within the seemingly insignificant moments are bliss. Your child getting into bed with you and snuggling up while it's cold outside. Children giggling with happiness. Blowing bubbles as the light catches them. A rainbow that comes when it rains. Swimming in the ocean when the sun is shining down on your face and feeling the warmth. Wrapping up and walking through the forest on a crisp, cold day, or a warm mug of tea with a good friend. Laughing with your friends or smiling at a happy memory. Hearing your favourite song and letting it transport you to that moment in an instant. These are the moments of bliss, and we miss them when we are always searching and wanting more. I have always pushed myself forward, but at the same time and for too long, I kept missing these moments as I was too busy trying to get that perfect place. *If I have this, I will be happy. If I get to that place in my business, I will be happy.* Instead, I should have realised that happiness is in the moment—the power of now is all we have—it really is as simple as that.

Everything Is in Your Grasp When You Start To Believe

How many times in your life have you wanted something so much but when you got it, or when you got there, you realised you weren't as happy at you thought you would be and then you start striving for something else? Or how many times have you wanted something so much, yet you let others dampen your dreams because of their issues or fears? How many times have you not lived your life because of others putting doubts and fears upon you? Like casting a magical spell over you in this book, my intention is to give you these tools so you can strip back everything. I want you to peel off the different layers, removing them one by one by one until you can see your golden light. You can then have everything you desire as you finally find your golden light hiding amongst the undergrowth. You can have all of it; all of it can be yours within this life—and you are worthy of it, every little thing.

As you go through your healing journey, I want you to honour everything you are and everything you desire to be. Know that many may try to stop you from doing this work. You may get some unkind and belittling comments, especially from the people who are closest to you. Believe me, I have had it all, but stand firm in who you are. This is your life. You came here alone, and you will leave this life alone, so it's important that you do you. Do not let others live their life through you. Shake it off, stand tall with your feet planted on the ground and go forth.

I have come up against lots of incorrect advice and negativity from some of the people closest to me over the years. I stood firm in my desire to live out my dreams, and it's only since I began to do this work that I realised the reason they tried to hold me back was nothing to do with me; it was that they had work to do, and I was triggering them. I would let myself feel the guilt and shame and start to question myself and my choices. Often the noise around me would be so loud that I would not live out some of my dreams. I hold no regrets, but I made a vow to myself years ago that I would live my life the way I was intended to do and make sure that as long as I check in with my heart and feel aligned, I would trust myself. I know that my feeling this way will allow my children to make only the choices in life they want—it is their blueprint and their journey. I feel that by their mother understanding and embodying this work, it gives them permission to live out their dreams too! I do not want to live my life through theirs. They are not my trophies and something shiny to be showed off at dinner parties. *They are here for themselves, and themselves only.* My biggest desire for them is that they live a life embodied in their truth.

Remembering Who You Are

Sometimes in the past other people's words and desires for me have shaken me a little, but I must trust that there is something bigger at play. I genuinely believe a power far greater than us is moving us through this life. We are going through a vast global awakening. So many people are starting to rise into the true versions of themselves. Remember, we are spiritual beings having a human experience. We were never intended to be separate from source energy. We were never created to be walking this life without guidance from our angels and guides. Through fear, conditioning, and control, those things have been removed from generations of humans as we entered the industrial age. But, now as our planet heads further to the light, we are all waking up and finding our inner light.

I would never have thought at the beginning of this book that Karl and I could have been even contemplating having another baby, and I had no idea that Seren would be contemplating moving schools. I have discovered through writing this book that I was holding on to a lot from my childhood and projecting it onto her. Travelling for seven weeks with the kids, we had some crazy, stressful moments with the children, but, I have found myself to be calmer than ever, breezing through two moon times and also learning not to enter the craziness when I am triggered by the children. This, for me, is huge, and it's only been possible when I began to heal.

What I have learned is that I allowed my children to heal me, and in turn, I was able to heal them. It's been truly magnificent to watch. I now understand that they were holding up a mirror for me, and when I honoured that and looked within, I was able to heal those parts of myself I was hiding. As I healed, so did they. What a miracle, what a gift, what a blessing. Seren was here to help me delve deep into my inner child; she helped me to work through my triggers and boundaries, and I became brave and began to speak my truth.

Daisy has helped me to work on my anger, again taking me through parts of my journey with my inner child and reaching to those parts that needed healing. I was finally able to sit with the shadows and shine the light on them. Flynn helped me to move through my guilt and shame. He has been an absolute pleasure to parent, but he also brought up self-love issues for me. Flynn has always been really attached to Karl. I guess he was the only baby where Karl was around a lot more, and he was really drawn to Karl. There have been many times when he wouldn't even want to come to me, and would only want Karl, especially when he was a toddler, and we were out with friends. Feelings of insecurity would pop-up, but remembering my self-love, self-acceptance, and a knowing and trusting in my heart would allow me to see how beautiful it was for Karl. What a gift to Karl, as his dad was never around because he worked abroad and then sadly, he left the family home when Karl was only 11 years old. Flynn has brought Karl so much love and healing. I am so truly happy for Karl and Flynn, as they have most the special bond.

I have no idea what another baby could bring, but we will have a completely different approach, and I will be writing about it in my next book. For those of you who have read my previous book or followed my journey on social media, you will know that I had two incredible homebirths. I practised Hypnobirthing with all three babies, but the one thing I didn't do was a conscious conception, which I will be doing this time. Then, of course, I will share it with the world!

I want you to know that whether you are planning on another baby or you are planning on conceiving your first baby, when we heal ourselves, we can stop own trauma or ancestral trauma being passed onto our babies. That is something we are not taught, and I find its kind of crazy! We are taught about the sperm and the egg. We are taught about periods and sex, but never are we taught about the sacred act of healing or of the sacred act of sex or even the sacredness of having a period. It's like all the richness and beauty has been taken from this magic of life and it has become so clinical. In many ways, such things such as when a woman bleeds, or we engage in making love or the taboo of self-pleasure, the Western World has injected shame around it, when it's something beautiful.

Your Womb Can Be A Portal of Light

Years ago, when I taught Hypnobirthing, I was fascinated by learning about Tibetan women and how they prepared for birth. They knew instinctively that they had to be ready for the baby, even before conception. They knew they needed to have healed their body. They understood that they needed to have healed their emotions and let go of anything that didn't serve them and prepare them for the birth of the baby. I never really understood the gift the Tibetan women gave to their children until now, and I feel so passionate that their way of conception and birth should be shared with all women.

As I have learned on this ever-changing journey of mother-hood, we are not taught in the Western World all we need to do to allow our babies to be born into our pool of light instead picking up all the emotional, physical, and spiritual debris as they enter the chalice of life. We are taught about pregnancy and birth, but even that instils fear into women instead of them honouring them during that most sacred time. What I have learned through parenting a spirited child and all the years of research is that we must prepare our bodies before conception like Tibetan women. We now understand by testing the umbilical cords of babies that, they have thousands of chemicals inside them. Our body is our babies' house, and it's such a gift to our babies if we can get rid of the toxins before we conceive—for both men and women. We need to eliminate our trauma and ancestral trauma, so it isn't passed on to our babies. Through meditation, we can even connect with the spirit of the baby to let them know we are ready for them. I can't believe it has taken me three babies to discover all this potent magic.

Trust the Journey

It's also essential you know that whatever happens was meant to happen. If you have a child or children already, you are meant to have your baby, this way, at this time. He or she was meant to be this way as there were lessons you needed to endure. If Seren hadn't been my spirited child, I would never have learned everything I have. I would never have understood my gifts that came through writing my books. I would never have learned how to meditate, which then lead me to channelling. I wouldn't change one thing about my journey, even if I could. I am so grateful for my amazing daughter, and even though she challenges me most days, I see within those challenges a need to heal something within myself. *Let us learn to be grateful for everything, even the things that drive us crazy, because herein lies our truth.*

The more I healed, the more my children healed. The deeper I allowed myself to go into my soul, the deeper I was able to go with my children and with Karl. I finally discovered that I had been co-dependant with Karl for almost twenty years, but through healing, I realised he wasn't on this earth to make me happy; only I could do that. The more I practised self-love, courage, and bravery, the more I was able to let go of the co-dependency, and our relationship became stronger. The more time I spent in meditation, the more I was able to tap into that beautiful, heart space and drown out the voice of my ego 'Glennis'. The more I did the work, the stronger I became, and the more I was able to finally find myself.

Listen to The Inner Knowings

We all have a dream; those niggling feelings deep within. I want you to listen to them and not let them be drowned out by the noise. Listen to your divine light calling you home. I want you to remember you are beautiful, you are worthy, and you are so much more than you ever realise. I am here to lovingly remind you that your life is a gift, and when you do the inner work, your light will become a magnet for more light. You will start to radiate so brightly that even the sun will need sunnies!

I want to remind you that the journey you are embarking upon is not for the faint-hearted, but you have the power inside of you to stop the generational curse. You have within you the magic to steer your future lineage on a completely different path. What a privilege and how incredible are you—don't ever forget it. Be so proud of yourself, and remember, at times we need to go through the darkness to get to the light. Don't be afraid during those times; keep putting one foot in front of the other and trust that you are deeply held as you do this work. Now is your time to heal, to awaken, to rise, and to shine your light out into the world.

I sat writing the final few hundred words of this book while my children were fighting and screaming in the background. I could have given in and given them their electronics, but I refused (they'd already been on them way too long). I was so absorbed in my words and my writing; it felt like I was in a magical world that didn't allow anything to permeate my writing bubble! With Flynn unable to go out as he's caught hand, foot, and mouth disease, Daisy proclaiming she was 'soooooo bored', and Seren trying to act like the mum and boss everyone around, I was somehow able to ignore the chaos that surrounded me. I even managed to dodge a few pencils thrown at me by Flynnie, who said I was the meanest mum in the world. Karl was out working (and squeezing in a cheeky surf), so I sat melting in the humid Bali heat. I couldn't stop my fingers from tapping on the keyboard. I felt like there was an invisible smoke coming off those badass fingers!

As the final few hundred words came flowing, I could feel it was the end drawing near; I sat crying as the last words entered the screen. All three children saw me blubbering and typing and came over to see what was wrong. 'I'm finishing my book, children', I told them. Seren gave me the biggest hug, told off everyone for being too loud, and the last few hundred words were birthed with my children next to me sitting and watching. Seren kept telling me over and over and again that she was so of proud me (sometimes I swear she is like the mum). Their little faces were watching me make a million spelling mistakes, and they were telling me that red lines meant I needed to go back and change the mistakes! As I finished with the final words I cried so much, but tears of joy and happiness, and to finish the book this way with my little people surrounding me was precisely the way the universe intended it to be. I have felt so held and supported writing this book, and I know it's been co-created with the universe.

Our Children Become Our Teachers

What a labour of love this book has been. This book has healed me in so many ways. It's allowed me to have some deep and sacred conversations with Karl, which I am sure will now change the course of our life. It's helped me to process some unhealed mum guilt and finally see that I give myself a hard time sometimes, but that's ok too—that is just the way this mama rolls! This book has allowed me to see why my children chose me. I was able to see what lessons they had for me, and how each of them came with a gift, an offering, and teaching for me. It has made me realise what a privilege we have as mothers, as we can change the course of our lineage. We don't have to continue with the generational curse. We can steer completely off course if we so wish and take it from the dark to the light. And yes, it may be messy, we may fuck up, and we may make mistakes along the process, but that's what makes life so beautiful. The beauty comes within the messiness. The rainbow only comes through the rain. It's ok when things don't go to plan. We are always divinely guided. I have shared so much in this book—my truth, my heart, my fears, my mess-ups, and my spiritual journey. I have pushed the metaphysical window with this book and shared some big stuff!

This book is for mamas but also mamas to be. I wish I had known how important it was to heal before we had our babies, how we needed to heal our unprocessed pain, trauma, and ancestral trauma, so it isn't passed down to our children. I wish I'd known that often our firstborn can take the biggest hit, so if you have a spirited child, love them hard, stop trying to fix them, and heal yourself—that is the way to healing them. Let love in and watch the transformation, and don't forget to have to fun along the way. Healing is beautiful, but so is your life. Don't take yourself too seriously, remember to laugh at yourself, and remember to honour the days when you look like a bag of poo because these are the days that count—because the imperfections are where the true beauty lies. Remember to have fun even when you are healing. Remember to dance naked in the rain, tilt back your head and drink the raindrops, swim in the ocean, walk around the house naked and proud with all your wobbly bits, and laugh until you wee yourself.

Remember that healing is important but so is living—so, make it count!

P.S. I'm pregnant!

CHAPTER 10
HEALING TOOLS FOR MAMA

Reading a book is one thing, but we need more if we want to allow the healing transformation to take place. You have inside of you the love, wisdom, and knowledge to heal. You just need the tools to help you remember. Once you learn to unlock the magic and the gift within, your healing will take you on the most beautiful and profound journey of your life. The light inside of you will radiate out to your children, partner, and even friends and family. The light inside of me honours the light inside of you.

This chapter will give you all the healing tools you need to walk you lovingly through this path. I have included eight different guided meditations I have written for you to help you move through each chapter, plus a powerful Inner Child meditation by Dr. Nicole LePera. I also have included some simple prayers that help me shift my energy and get clarity.

I have included books that have helped me on my journey as well as other healing modalities such as breathwork, reiki, and psych-K. This chapter is packed full of additional resources for you, and I included a beautiful Spotify playlist to help you awaken and heal.

Dr. Nicole LePera has given you an in-depth overview of how to start future-self journalling over the next 30 days. I know if you begin this daily practise you will see significant changes in your life! I am so excited for you!

Buckle up, sister; this is going to be a beautiful ride!

Guided Meditations

All the guided meditations can also be found here; www.susyohare.com/mother

- Cutting Chords with Archangel Michael meditation—https://susyparker.s3-ap-southeast-2.amazonaws.com/Cutting+Chords+Guided+Meditation.mp3
- The Triggers Are The Guides meditation—https://susyparker.s3-ap-southeast-2.amazonaws.com/The+Triggers+are+the+guides+meditation.mp3
- Letting Go Meditation—https://susyparker.s3-ap-southeast-2.amazonaws.com/Letting+Go+Guided+Meditation+For+Women.mp3
- Chakra Cleansing Meditation—https://susyparker.s3-ap-southeast-2.amazonaws.com/Chakra+Cleansing+-Meditation.mp3
- Grounding Meditation—https://susyparker.s3-ap-southeast-2.amazonaws.com/Grounding+Meditation.mp3
- Releasing The Heaviness meditation—https://susyparker.s3-ap-southeast-2.amazonaws.com/Release+The+Heaviness+-+11_3_19%2C+1.41+pm+1.mp3
- Shedding Our Skin meditation—https://susyparker.s3-ap-southeast-2.amazonaws.com/Shedding+Our+Skin+-+11%3A3%3A19%2C+2.10+pm.mp3
- Manifesting New Moon Ritual—https://susyparker.s3-ap-southeast-2.amazonaws.com/New+Moon+Ritual.mp3
- Boundaries Meditation—https://susyparker.s3-ap-southeast-2.amazonaws.com/Boundaries+Meditation.mp3

Prayers

Prayer for Releasing Negative Energy

Dear Archangel Michael, please release any negativity I may have picked up, and release it back to the light. Please return any of the energy I may have lost and bring it back to me. Thank you.

Morning and/or Evening Prayer (from A Course in Miracles by Helen Schucman)

I say this prayer most evenings as I lie in bed, just before going to sleep.

Dear God, Where would you have me go? What would you have me do? What would you have me say, and to whom?

Prayer for Clarity

For this one, I tend to kneel on the ground, place my hands together in the prayer position, close my eyes and say this prayer out loud repeatedly. I have found that I often get instant clarity with this prayer.

Dear God/Universe, Teach me. Guide me. Heal me.

Prayer For Instant Guidance

Universe/God, please show me the tools I need to work on my healing. Please bring me what I need in this moment. I trust all that comes my way. Thank you.

Books

- *The Dance of Anger: A Woman's Guide To Changing The Patterns Of Intimate Relationships* by Harriet Lerner Ph.D.
- *The Power of Now: A Guide to Spiritual Enlightenment* by Eckhart Tolle
- *A New Earth: Awakening to Your Life's Purpose* by Eckhart Tolle

- *You Can Heal Your Life* by Louise Hay
- *Dying To Be Me: My Journey from Cancer, to Near Death, to True Healing* by Anita Moorjani
- *Totem Animals Plain & Simple: The Only Book You'll Ever Need* (Plain & Simple Series) by Celia M Gunn
- *The Dream Interpretation Dictionary: Symbols, Signs, and Meanings* by J.M. Debord
- *Healing Back Pain: The Mind Body Connection* by John E Sarno, M.D.

Mantras

I have included mantras for you which I have infused through-out the book; you will see these on many of the pages. If you feel one that resonates with your soul, it will help you to activate the light within you. Pop the message on a Post-It® note and place it on your bathroom mirror so you may see it each day.

Susy's Spotify Playlist

Susy's Spotify list can also be found here;
www.susyohare.com/mother

Playlist For your Healing Journey:
https://open.spotify.com/playlist/0fEkN7bcpYVEPmamzQ
oeEs?si=_oQv3-5JQ_e7rvjSaOpXog

Healing Your Body and Mind Naturally

The interview can also be found here;
www.susyohare.com/mother

Interview with leading child healthcare experts, Dr. Natalie Challis (neuropsychotherapist) and Leigh Shinde (nutritionist):
https://www.instagram.com/tv/Bwt7QwAjDhQ/

Additional Healing Resources

All the additional healing resources can also be found here; www.susyohare.com/mother

EFT (Tapping)
- Brad Yates is a renowned EFT teacher with many free EFT videos on his YouTube channel. https://tapwithbrad. mykajabi.com/
- Nick Ortner is the founder of The Tapping Solution. He and his sister, Jessica Ortner, have written several books on EFT. https://www.thetappingsolution.com/

Trauma Therapists
- The EMDR International Association to find a trained therapist https://www.emdria.org/about-emdr-therapy/

Other Healing Modalities and Resources

All the other healing modalities and resources can also be found here; www.susyohare.com/mother

- Psych K Internationalhttps://psych-k.com/
- Human Givens - https://www.hgi.org.uk/
- Breathwork - https://ibfbreathwork.org/
- Reiki - https://www.reiki.org/faqs/what-reiki
- Sound Healing - Sound Healing - https://www.healthline. com/health/sound-healing
- Awaken: A Conscious Social Media App - https://awaken. app/
- How My Spiritual Journey Is Healing My PMDD https://www.youtube.com/watch?v=_mSWaTGMrqw
- *In Utero* Film - https://www.inuterofilm.com/

Future-Self Journalling by Dr. Nicole LePera

This practise literally changed my life, which is why I would love you to try and commit to this practise for at least 30 days. You only need about ten minutes a day, but I promise you will begin to have some incredibly powerful and positive results from this! Dr. LePera guides you below on how to use future-self journalling and covers any questions you might have.

What is future-self journalling?

Future-self journalling works because it creates conscious awareness around your behaviours and patterns. For many of us, this exercise is the first (and only time) we've done this. Subconscious literally means below awareness. It's the mental software created in our childhood while our brain was in a theta hypnotic state. We needed this mental software to learn how to 'be' in our world. As children, we had to quickly learn the language, social norms, how to communicate, and what was expected of us from our caregivers. We didn't get to choose consciously what beliefs and behaviours we wanted to adopt. They were chosen for us.

By age seven, we became conscious as our brain waves shifted. We continued to operate under this mental software, unaware of its existence.

Every time we are doing something without being fully present, the subconscious is running. We run on autopilot. Think about your drive to work. Your mind may be thinking about what you'll do that day at work or the fight you had with your partner the previous night. Yet, you're making all the right turns. You're braking at red lights and driving when you see green. The subconscious is at work. When you start paying attention, you'll see just how often you are in this state.

To change our behaviour, we must become conscious of our subconscious routine. By being present and aware of our habit loops, we can start to shift them.

Future-self journalling is a tool that allows you to start becoming conscious. The more you use it, the more your consciousness will expand. It's in this expanded consciousness state where you find the ultimate empowerment: choice in response.

How do I begin?

You begin with 'self-awareness'. This step is only done once for each habit you want to work to change or develop. You use this format to find the behavioural patterns you want to change. Note: I do get messages from some people who can't figure out what it is they want to change. That means you need to observe yourself before you can begin. If you don't know what you want to change, start your day with this intention: 'Today, I will notice behaviours that are holding me back from my highest potential'. Do this for one to two weeks. Write down (or enter the notepad on your phone) the insights as you get them. Then, you can begin Step 1.

Step 1: Self-Awareness

I will go through some examples below:

1. What behaviour or pattern do I want to change? Focus on one.

   'I want to stop becoming defensive in my day to day interactions.'

2. Write affirmations or statements that will help you achieve this. Let them flow naturally. Do not over-think it.

   I can hear other perspectives I am calm. I create space between my reaction. I am safe within my body.

3. Write about how you will be able to practise these new behaviours in daily life.

I will practise observing the feelings and thoughts that come up rather than habitually reacting when interacting with my family.

After you're finished Step 1, you don't need to complete it again for at least 30 days or until you see successful change. Then you can start working on a new pattern. You will now go onto Step 2.

Step 2: My daily affirmation: (I will include examples below)

I am calm and peaceful. I can observe and not react.

Today I will focus on shifting my pattern of habitually reacting to situations when facing an emotional trigger.

I am grateful for the opportunity to become a different version of myself, my pets, my family, the ability to create, and my favourite hiking trail.

The person I am becoming will experience more joy, gratitude, abundance, and the ability to live in the present moment.

I have an opportunity to be my future-self today when I pause and listen rather than react.

When I think about who I am becoming, I feel confident, fulfilled, proud of my healing.

The Most Frequently Asked Questions about future-self journalling.

Do I need to do it every single day?

Yes. This technique uses neuroplasticity. Our brains are elastic, which means through intentional acts, we can change the pathways in our mind. However, it takes consistent repetition to change these pathways. This practise only takes five to eight minutes a day which makes it easy to complete daily.

What if I skip a day?

No problem. If you skip a day, that is not an issue. Try to avoid assigning meaning to skipping a day (i.e., I never finish what I start or I'm lazy). Affirm to yourself that you will start again tomorrow. With each new habit, there are times when we will not show up. That is part of the path of learning to trust yourself. Today is one day. Tomorrow is a new opportunity.

I have major resistance to journalling. I can't seem to start. Help.

Resistance (mental chatter) is very normal. We typically have resistance to the things we need to do most for our evolution. The subconscious mind is very powerful, and when we attempt to break up its patterning, there will be a mental temper tantrum. You might feel anxious, scared, or even completely blocked off from doing it. Overcoming this is part of the process. Each time you make a choice to do the practise even though your thoughts may be yelling not to, you are overcoming your mental resistance.

Don't focus on it being perfect or whether you are doing it right. If you can only do one question, just do one question. Build up each day. The act of completing a task you've committed to will be helpful in your healing.

What is the best/right time of day?

This is different for everyone. Some of you might want to do it before bed or first thing in the morning. Others might like to do it during a lunch break. The time is unimportant. It is the act of completing that is important. You might want to experiment with a few different times to see what works best. There is no 'right' time to do future-self journalling.

I am not having any breakthroughs. Does future-self journalling work for everyone?

Future-self journalling can work for everyone. It's the act of becoming consciously aware. However, it's just a pathway to that awareness. You will start to be more aware of how you're thinking and behaving. The more you commit to the practise without judging the experience, the better your results will be. Expectations around a 'breakthrough' might be blocking your awareness.

I don't want to keep the same pattern for 30 days. Can I change it?

You will get the most benefit if you stick to one pattern. It will allow you to focus your full attention on making that one change. You'll want to try to stick it out for at least the entire 30 days to ensure you are well on your way to saving this new habit as a new subconscious pattern.

I'm sceptical about this working

That is mental resistance, and it's normal. Don't focus on being sceptical. Focus your awareness on the questions. Answer them with as much clarity as you can. As you go through the process, the sceptical resistance will fade.

Is it ok if I type the future-self journal?

Yes. But you will get more benefit from writing the journal in longhand. Neuroscience shows us that writing connects differently in our brains.

I'm struggling with _____. What should I journal about?

You might come up against mental and emotional blocks during this process. Figuring out this process on your own is an important part of healing. Don't worry about doing it perfectly. Focus on connecting to your own inner voice.

AFTERWORD

This book has healed me on a deep cellular level. It has been a labour of love that began with an awakening that at times felt like a breakdown. But within the metamorphosis, I found myself hidden underneath the emotional, physical, and spiritual debris of my past lineage, and I began to heal. I finally said goodbye to the cocoon that was holding me back, stretched out my wings and began to fly. I discovered that with these new wings, I was able to see and experience life from a different lens which was a lens of love.

It has been a wild ride, and at times, I felt like I was losing my footing, but trusting and putting one step in front of the other, I continued forth into the unknown. One of the most beautiful things for me was to see the difference between Karl and my children. I prayed and hoped that Karl would also awaken, but it needed to happen at the right time. As I began to do the work and heal, I could see that he also needed it, but in a different way. I needed deep radical healing and self-acceptance; he needed to stop carrying his father's wounds, find his inner softness, and ascend into his true self. Witnessing my transformation has been amazing, but seeing Karl awaken has been such an honour.

The light inside of me was able to see the light inside of him, and together after twenty years, we were able to live in love without my co-dependency that had been hanging around like a heavy cloud. We were able to raise our children consciously and to see the difference in them is such a gift. They feel seen, heard, and held, and there is nothing I want to change about them. To us, they are perfect and as they should be. Our children are not on this earth for us to live our lives through them. They are here for their own true, divine reason. I feel that the most magical thing to come from writing this book is the gift of peace. I no longer yearn for a relationship with my birth mother. I am genuinely grateful that she gave me life, and I have been able to see the gifts she gave me and finally let go of the pain.

After yearning for another baby for the last six years, it is miraculous that I am writing these words with my beautiful baby moving around inside my belly. I am 22 weeks pregnant, and at 43, this has been the most wonderful, easy, and incredible pregnancy yet. If I hadn't broken free of the conditioning and fear, I would never have decided to have another baby. Remember what I said—live your life the way you want, girl! You are beholden to only yourself. Please hold that in your heart, always.

Writing this book and sharing my words, feelings, and thoughts helped and inspired Karl to go on his journey of healing. He was able to soften and say with a deep love and reverence that he would love another baby. That only happened when he realised the true gift of life and that our reason to incarnate on this earth is to love and give love. As soon as he gave me his blessing for another baby, I was pregnant the very next month. I feel like our spirit baby waited for this very moment. She wasn't meant to come into this world like Seren or my other children with keys to unlock my pain and trauma; she was meant to come here for an extraordinary reason, which I am yet to discover.

My wish for you is that you use the tools, mantras, prayers, meditations, and guidance to come home to your true self. I want to help you peel back the layers to unearth your light. I want you to stand in your true authentic self without the fear, conditioning, and generational trauma. Once you learn to unlock the magic and the gift within, your healing will take you on the most beautiful and profound journey of your life. This light inside of you will radiate out to your children, partner, and even further than you may be able to comprehend. Your light truly can reach the cosmos!

Because you, my dear, have no idea how powerful you really are! Never forget you are made of stardust! You have the moon, stars, and galaxies infused into the fabric of your soul. So, shine bright like the diamond that you are, and may you never, ever dim your light again.

ACKNOWLEDGEMENTS

I want to first give thanks to my incredible children for all the magic and the lessons you have brought to me. I am beyond grateful that you chose me to be your mama, and I love you all to the moon and back. I want to thank my life partner and soul mate, Karl, for this incredible awakened life that we have co-created. After twenty years, I still count my lucky stars every day that our paths crossed; I love you so much.

Thank you to my awesome dad for letting me share some of your life in this book. I truly believe we were meant to share our story, as it will go on to help others, and I am eternally grateful that you gave me your blessing.

Endless thanks to my editor, Gailyc, for helping me craft this book yet enabling me to keep my voice. Thank you to my lovely friend, Bronnie, for all the photography over the last few years. Big love to every person, friend, family member, and healer who has helped me in my life to be the person I am today. What a ride it's been!

Susy O'Hare

Susy is an author, meditation teacher, speaker and mama to three (soon to be four) amazing children. Susy's writing first began after she published her first book, *Diary of an ADHD Mum: Learning to Live, Love & Laugh Parenting a Child with ADHD.*

Susy is passionate about empowering parents to accept the child they have and to make peace with their child's differences. She empowers mothers to tap into their intuition, step out of a lens of fear, and parent through a lens of love.

Susy feels passionately that instead of trying to heal the child, we must allow ourselves to witness that our child is our mirror. Only then can we let the triggers guide us to our unhealed, unprocessed pain, and trauma. Susy teaches mothers that to heal their child, first, they must heal themselves, and she gives them the tools to do this potent and life-transforming work.

Susy has been featured as a guest writer for blogs such as *Lifehack, Healthline,* and *ADDitude Magazine,* as well as being interviewed on various podcasts. Susy has been featured in both local and national newspapers, magazines, and mainstream television in Australia.

Keep up to date with Susy at www.susyohare.com.

Dr Nicole LePera

Dr. Nicole LePera is a Holistic Psychologist who believes that mental wellness is for everyone. She evolved her more traditional training from Cornell University and The New School to one that acknowledges the connection between the mind and body.

Dr. LePera views mental and physical struggles from a whole person perspective and works to identify the underlying physical and emotional causes. She understands that balance is an integral part of wellness and empowers individuals to heal themselves, supporting them on their wellness journeys.

Dr. LePera founded the Mindful Healing Centre in Centre City Philadelphia. She recently expanded her work online to create a platform for teaching these often-overlooked components of mental wellness to individuals and practitioners around the world.

Operation Underground Railroad

A portion of the proceeds from each book is donated to Operation Underground Railroad. This is a cause that Susy feels very passionate about. She feels that by shining the light on sex trafficking, together we can make a difference to the children of this world.

O.U.R. is a non-profit organization whose mission is to eradicate child sex trafficking. Because this problem is so vast, they have gathered the world's experts in both extraction operations and in anti-child trafficking with a goal of bringing an end to child slavery.

O.U.R. enlists Jump Team members with experience in anti-trafficking and extraction operations with the goal of rescuing trafficked children and identifying those who enslave them. Jump Team consists of current and former CIA, Navy SEALs, law enforcement officers and Special Ops personnel who coordinate rescue efforts with foreign governments and law enforcement partners throughout the world.

O.U.R's aftercare develops partnerships with vetted in-country aftercare centres. Once victims are rescued, the recovery process begins. They also provide vocational training where possible to survivors around the world.

O.U.R. provide support to other NGOs around the world and exchanges ideas, methods and best practices. They are amazing organizations doing such great work in this fight and O.U.R. believe in coming together to save children anywhere possible.

For more information, to support or donate, please visit www.OURrescue.org.

Lightning Source UK Ltd.
Milton Keynes UK
UKHW011119021120
372651UK00001B/194